TEENAGE SEXUALITY

Opposing Viewpoints®

Other Books of Related Interest in the Opposing Viewpoints Series:

Abortion
Male/Female Roles
The Mass Media
Sexual Values

Additional Books in the Opposing Viewpoints Series:

AIDS
American Foreign Policy
American Government
The American Military
American Values
America's Elections
America's Prisons
The Arms Race
Biomedical Ethics
Censorship
Central America
Chemical Dependency
Civil Liberties
Constructing a Life Philosophy
Crime & Criminals
Criminal Justice
Death and Dying
The Death Penalty
Drug Abuse
Economics in America
The Environmental Crisis
Latin America
The Middle East
Nuclear War
The Political Spectrum
Poverty
Problems of Africa
Science and Religion
Social Justice
The Soviet Union
Terrorism
The Vietnam War
War and Human Nature

TEENAGE SEXUALITY

Opposing Viewpoints®

David L. Bender & Bruno Leone, *Series Editors*

Neal Bernards, *Book Editor*
Lynn Hall, *Assistant Editor*

OPPOSING VIEWPOINTS SERIES ®

Greenhaven Press, Inc.   P.O. Box 289009   San Diego, CA 92128-9009

Library of Congress Cataloging-in-Publication Data

Teenage sexuality.

(Opposing viewpoints series)
Bibliography: p.
Includes index.
Summary: Presents opposing viewpoints about teenage attitudes toward sex, their sexual and reproductive rights, teenage pregnancy, sex education, and school-based clinics.
  1. Teenagers—United States—Sexual behavior.
2. Sex instruction for teenagers—United States.
3. Teenage pregnancy—United States. 4. Birth control clinics—United States. [1. Sex instruction for youth. 2. Sexual ethics. 3. Pregnancy.
4. Birth control] I. Bernards, Neal, 1963-

II. Hall, Lynn, 1949-   . III. Series.
HQ27.T425 1988   306.7'088055   87-37268
ISBN 0-89908-405-2 (pbk.)
ISBN 0-89908-430-3 (lib. bdg.)

"Congress shall make no law . . . abridging the freedom of speech, or of the press."

First Amendment to the US Constitution

The basic foundation of our democracy is the first amendment guarantee of freedom of expression. The *Opposing Viewpoints Series* is dedicated to the concept of this basic freedom and the idea that it is more important to practice it than to enshrine it.

Contents

Why Consider Opposing Viewpoints?

"It is better to debate a question without settling it than to settle a question without debating it."

Joseph Joubert (1754-1824)

The Importance of Examining Opposing Viewpoints

The purpose of the Opposing Viewpoints Series, and this book in particular, is to present balanced, and often difficult to find, opposing points of view on complex and sensitive issues.

Probably the best way to become informed is to analyze the positions of those who are regarded as experts and well studied on issues. It is important to consider every variety of opinion in an attempt to determine the truth. Opinions from the mainstream of society should be examined. But also important are opinions that are considered radical, reactionary, or minority as well as those stigmatized by some other uncomplimentary label. An important lesson of history is the eventual acceptance of many unpopular and even despised opinions. The ideas of Socrates, Jesus, and Galileo are good examples of this.

Readers will approach this book with their own opinions on the issues debated within it. However, to have a good grasp of one's own viewpoint, it is necessary to understand the arguments of those with whom one disagrees. It can be said that those who do not completely understand their adversary's point of view do not fully understand their own.

A persuasive case for considering opposing viewpoints has been presented by John Stuart Mill in his work *On Liberty*. When examining controversial issues it may be helpful to reflect on this suggestion:

> The only way in which a human being can make some approach to knowing the whole of a subject, is by hearing what can be said about it by persons of every variety of opinion, and studying all modes in which it can be looked at by every character of mind. No wise man ever acquired his wisdom in any mode but this.

Analyzing Sources of Information

The Opposing Viewpoints Series includes diverse materials taken from magazines, journals, books, and newspapers, as well as statements and position papers from a wide range of individuals, organizations and governments. This broad spectrum of sources helps to develop patterns of thinking which are open to the consideration of a variety of opinions.

Pitfalls To Avoid

A pitfall to avoid in considering opposing points of view is that of regarding one's own opinion as being common sense and the most rational stance and the point of view of others as being only opinion and naturally wrong. It may be that another's opinion is correct and one's own is in error.

Another pitfall to avoid is that of closing one's mind to the opinions of those with whom one disagrees. The best way to approach a dialogue is to make one's primary purpose that of understanding the mind and arguments of the other person and not that of enlightening him or her with one's own solutions. More can be learned by listening than speaking.

It is my hope that after reading this book the reader will have a deeper understanding of the issues debated and will appreciate the complexity of even seemingly simple issues on which good and honest people disagree. This awareness is particularly important in a democratic society such as ours where people enter into public debate to determine the common good. Those with whom one disagrees should not necessarily be regarded as enemies, but perhaps simply as people who suggest different paths to a common goal.

Developing Basic Reading and Thinking Skills

In this book, carefully edited opposing viewpoints are purposely placed back to back to create a running debate; each viewpoint is preceded by a short quotation that best expresses the author's main argument. This format instantly plunges the reader into the midst of a controversial issue and greatly aids that reader in mastering the basic skill of recognizing an author's point of view.

A number of basic skills for critical thinking are practiced in the activities that appear throughout the books in the series. Some of the skills are:

Evaluating Sources of Information The ability to choose from among alternative sources the most reliable and accurate source in relation to a given subject.

Separating Fact from Opinion The ability to make the basic distinction between factual statements (those that can be demonstrated or verified empirically) and statements of opinion (those that are beliefs or attitudes that cannot be proved).

Identifying Stereotypes The ability to identify oversimplified, exaggerated descriptions (favorable or unfavorable) about people and insulting statements about racial, religious or national groups, based upon misinformation or lack of information.

Recognizing Ethnocentrism The ability to recognize attitudes or opinions that express the view that one's own race, culture, or group is inherently superior, or those attitudes that judge another culture or group in terms of one's own.

It is important to consider opposing viewpoints and equally important to be able to critically analyze those viewpoints. The activities in this book are designed to help the reader master these thinking skills. Statements are taken from the book's viewpoints and the reader is asked to analyze them. This technique aids the reader in developing skills that not only can be applied to the viewpoints in this book, but also to situations where opinionated spokespersons comment on controversial issues. Although the activities are helpful to the solitary reader, they are most useful when the reader can benefit from the interaction of group discussion.

Using this book and others in the series should help readers develop basic reading and thinking skills. These skills should improve the reader's ability to understand what they read. Readers should be better able to separate fact from opinion, substance from rhetoric and become better consumers of information in our media-centered culture.

This volume of the Opposing Viewpoints Series does not advocate a particular point of view. Quite the contrary! The very nature of the book leaves it to the reader to formulate the opinions he or she finds most suitable. My purpose as publisher is to see that this is made possible by offering a wide range of viewpoints which are fairly presented.

David L. Bender
Publisher

Introduction

"Sex oozes from every pore of the culture and there's not a kid in the world who can avoid it."

Charles Krauthammer

Sex permeates US society. From pop music to prime-time television, sex fills the fantasy world of entertainment and advertising. The fantasy does not precisely mirror reality, however. Adolescents face the threat of sexually-transmitted diseases, psychological pressure to have sex earlier than ever before, and a devastating rate of pregnancy. According to the Alan Guttmacher Institute, a research organization involved in reproductive health care, 1.2 million teens become pregnant each year. This sobering statistic sparks debate over how to solve the problems surrounding teenage sexuality. The focal point of this controversy concerns the message society should convey to teens about sex and the manner in which this message should be relayed.

A popular slogan urges America's youth to "just say no" to peer pressure concerning sex. Supporters of the "just say no" philosophy maintain that abstinence from premarital sex is the only sane alternative in an era of AIDS, herpes, and unplanned pregnancies. They also believe that society's costs from teenage pregnancy are a tremendous burden. Of all women under age thirty who receive Aid to Families with Dependent Children (AFDC), seventy-one percent gave birth to their first child while still teenagers. Only fifty percent of the young women who have children before age eighteen finish high school. Supporters of abstinence believe that, moral questions aside, these statistics are evidence that teens should be discouraged from engaging in sexual activity.

Many health care officials and teachers, however, argue that rather than deny that over fifty percent of all seventeen-year-olds have had sexual intercourse, adults should teach America's youth to make intelligent decisions about their sexuality. They believe it is naive to assume that teenagers will simply end their sexual activity. Instead, they advocate programs which provide teens with access to contraception, abortion, and treatment of sexual diseases.

Sex educators cite studies done on adolescent fertility to support their arguments. According to one study, the youth of Sweden and the Netherlands are as sexually active as American youth, but have barely one-third the pregnancy rate and a much lower incidence of sexually-transmitted disease. This is due, researchers say, to excellent sex education programs that begin in grade school and continue throughout the school-age years. By openly discussing sex and making adolescents responsible for their behavior, they argue, Swedish and Dutch sex educators have successfully dealt with the consequences of teenage sexual activity.

Another controversy over teenage sexuality focuses on who should teach adolescents about sexual matters. Most health-care experts agree that parents could be the ideal sex educators. Unfortunately, many parents are uncomfortable discussing sex with their children and some do not relay accurate information. The public schools are often viewed as the next logical choice for sex education, but many religious leaders object to what they consider the schools' amoral approach to the subject. By default, it seems, the job of informing many teens about sex is often left to their peers and the mass media. Sexual myths abound among teenagers due to misinformation and their peers' exaggerated tales of sexual exploits. Equally misleading messages about sex are portrayed in the mass media, which use sex to sell products, improve television ratings, and increase box office receipts.

In *Teenage Sexuality: Opposing Viewpoints*, authors debate the following topics: What Affects Teenagers' Attitudes Toward Sex? What Kind of Sex Education Is Appropriate for Teenagers? Are School-Based Health Clinics Beneficial? How Can the Teenage Pregnancy Problem Be Solved? and Should Teenagers Make Their Own Sexual Decisions? The issue of how to solve the problems surrounding teenage sexual activity will not be resolved easily but will remain in the forefront of problems concerning America's youth.

What Affects Teenagers' Attitudes Toward Sex?

TEENAGE SEXUALITY

Chapter Preface

America's youth are inundated by sexual messages. Advertisements use sex to sell products. Television programs titillate audiences with steamy sex-filled plots. Parents warn children to be careful of sex. Religious leaders tell youth to abstain.

A pressing question in the debate over teenage sexuality is, what factor plays the greatest role in influencing teen attitudes? Is it the mass media and advertising? The family? Peers? Religion? Or is it a factor that sexual behaviorists have not yet discovered?

This chapter offers alternative theories about which factors are most important in affecting teenage sexuality.

"Sexual behavior is intertwined with issues of education, economics, politics, national security and employment."

Many Factors Affect Teenage Sexuality

Allen J. Moore

Allen J. Moore is the dean at the School of Theology in Claremont, California. In the following viewpoint, Moore writes that teenage sexuality is affected by many social and political factors beyond the control of adolescents. Moore maintains that teens did not create the sexual revolution, but inherited it from their grandparents and great-grandparents. He believes that teenage sexual behavior is influenced by economic status, societal values, and the accuracy of their knowledge concerning sex.

As you read, consider the following questions:

1. What examples does the author give to prove that social factors influence teenage sexual behavior?
2. Why does Moore believe it is counterproductive to teach moral absolutes regarding sex?
3. In the author's opinion, why is sexual ignorance dangerous?

We are a sexually active society, and teen-agers are no exception. The Moral Right may have won some battles at the ballot box, but there is little evidence that those victories have led to more restrictive sexual behavior. Evidence suggests that even the rise of AIDS has not resulted in a major shift in sexual habits. Rather than reinforcing a moral emphasis upon abstinence, AIDS has shifted concern to what is called "safe sex": increased care in choosing sexual partners, along with the habitual use of condoms. Most teen-agers are not yet preoccupied with AIDS, but the public discussion of it has brought talk of sexuality and contraceptives out in the open.

What is often overlooked in discussions of teen-age sexuality is that the young are not the creators of the sexual revolution. Rather, they are the recipients of a sexual heritage that actually dates to the turn of the century. As the Kinsey studies demonstrated (1948 and 1953), the sexual revolution in fact began with the generation born after 1900 (with the most far-reaching changes occurring among women). It was the great-grandmothers of today's teen-agers who ushered in more liberal views of sexuality.

Intertwining Factors

Sexual practices can never be examined and understood independently of other social factors. Moralists often do not recognize the complex ways in which sexual behavior is intertwined with issues of education, economics, politics, national security and employment. For example, the mothers of the vast majority of the children born out of wedlock are racial minority teen-agers who come from broken families living below the poverty level. Most of these teen-age mothers were themselves children of unmarried mothers. To take another example, women's greater sexual freedom is in part due to improved birth-control methods, which have given women the ability to separate their sexual desires from reproduction. The sexual liberation of women can also be correlated with their struggle for political freedom and social equality.

There are, however, particular ethical issues related to teen-age sexuality that need to be addressed. Teen-agers are not morally ready to make decisions about sexual intercourse. They generally are not emotionally ready to make judgments about the quality of intimate relationships, and they have not reached a level of maturity to take responsibility for their actions. The sociological evidence on abandonment, furthermore, makes it clear that teen-agers are not prepared to take social and economic responsibility for the birth of a baby.

Young people today are socially pressured to be sexually active long before they have been prepared educationally and psychologically to cope with the deeply personal and highly charged nature of sexuality. The mass media are filled with romantic images of male-female relationships, and the myth prevails that "to be carried away" by one's sexual urges is a sure sign of love, which justifies sexual interaction. Just as serious is the way our society's images of being male and being female demean the larger moral significance of sexuality. A teen-age boy faces the social pressure to "score" and, in so doing, he reduces his partner to a sexual object. And a teen-age girl absorbs the idea that a woman is someone who is sexually desirable to a man; her worth lies in her value as a sexual commodity and her ability to control the male with the sexual favors she provides.

Sexual morality in our time must address these factors underlying teen-age behavior. Sexual morality needs to offer a clear articulation of the meaning of interpersonal love and the need for justice in all aspects of human life. Youth need to know that sex does not need to be the determinant force in human life. . . .

Sources of Information

Kids seem to know a lot more about sex than they used to. If not from their families, or from the schools, . . . where are they getting it?

From their friends—some of whom know less than they do, and most of whom are (sometimes grossly) misinformed. From the media—movies, magazines, radio (including "rock" lyrics), and television, and even from the ubiquitous graffiti.

Irving R. Dickman, *Winning the Battle for Sex Education*, 1982.

A study by the Search Institute of Minneapolis indicates that one in five ninth graders has had sexual intercourse. Such early involvement in sexual activity correlates with other factors such as low achievement in school, little involvement in nurturing groups, and the family's inability to provide adequate emotional support. The rate of pregnancy among unmarried teen-age females is much higher among minorities and persons living in poverty than among whites and middle-class teens. A pregnant teen-age girl is thus often caught in a social and economic web that is a greater factor in her behavior than are all the moral absolutes she may have been taught (though many of these girls receive little or no such moral instruction). Such a girl is usually naive about sexuality and birth control, and has had little opportunity to take charge of her own body. She almost never seeks prenatal care, is often unaware of how to prepare for the birth, and is unlikely to have help in rearing the child (i.e., the father will very likely not be on the scene).

These findings do not suggest that white and middle-class teens are not sexually active, but that birth-control and family-planning services are generally more available to them. While it is true that 80 to 90 per cent of all births out of wedlock are to black teenagers, and that half of all black children live in female-headed families, it is also the case that black males form the largest unemployed group in the total population, and are the lowest-paid of employed males. The cycle of single motherhood within black communities is related to the ways in which minorities continue to be marginalized in our society, and continue to live at the poverty level. White teen-agers, especially of the middle class, more often have available to them the social resources by which the consequences of their sexual activity can be minimized, either through abortion or adoption. (We should note that black children born out of wedlock are seldom adopted. In some communities there are 40 times more black children than white children available for adoption.)

The Effects of Social Policy

The "profamily" policies of the [Reagan] administration are designed to take away public support from those who are most in need of social and medical services. The programs adhere to the middle-class ideology which sees each family as sufficient for meeting its own needs. What is missing from this view is a sense of a larger community in which the welfare of all persons is a shared responsibility. Repeated efforts are made to regulate sexual behavior by punitive measures, such as the "squeal" regulation that would require a medical facility to inform parents when an underage girl seeks medical help if she is pregnant or if she wants to obtain contraceptives. A similar invasion of civil rights is implicit in the initiative to require doctors to report to the Department of Health persons infected with the AIDS virus, and in the proposed restrictions that would prohibit any family planning institution receiving federal funds from informing clients of the availability of abortion services.

These legal efforts are not designed to help people develop positive attitudes about sexuality or to take more responsibility for their sexual behavior. Instead they impose punishment by withdrawing human services that could help people to cope more effectively with problems arising from their sexuality.

Policies based on negatives are irresponsible, particularly in an age in which we have so much knowledge and understanding of human sexuality. One aspect of these restrictive policies is the belief that sex is inherently wrong and that individuals should be left with the consequences of their "mistake." Such a basis for public policy is not consistent with either a humanitarian tradition or a Christian view, nor does it acknowledge the diversity of beliefs that exist concerning the role of sex in human life.

The policies of the profamily program are based on the idea that the problems arising from teen-age sexual activity are moral rather

20

than social. The approach that the U.S. Department of Health and Human Services is taking toward teen pregnancy is that premarital sex is morally wrong and that the best prevention is sexual abstinence. Title XX—the "chastity" law—passed by Congress in 1981 provides funds to groups, including certain church groups, that support programs of sexual abstinence among youth.

Accurate and Inaccurate Sources

By the time one reaches adolescence, the major source of sexual information and behavior reinforcement is provided by the peer group, with the media becoming an increasingly preferred source. The information provided by friends and the media, however, is often inaccurate. In a study by [H.D.] Thornburg (1974) it was found that students received the most accurate information (on venereal disease, abortion and menstruation, respectively) from school, literature, and their mothers; and the least accurate information (on homosexuality, intercourse, and masturbation) from their peers.

Andrea Parrot, *Human Sexuality*, 1984.

A growing coalition of conservative political leaders, religious groups and government officials is leading the attack against publicly supported programs of sex education, school-based health centers, guidance programs in family planning, and other activities designed to address the sexual needs of youth from both a social and a health perspective. Operating under the myth that sexual involvement is always delayed until marriage and that the family is the only normal setting for child-rearing, this coalition opposes programs of "optional parenthood" in which having a child is a matter of choice rather than of chance. The coalition is also unwilling to recognize the extent to which young people are engaged in sexual activity and the need they have for more accurate information and guidance in making sexual decisions. Gary Bauer, undersecretary of education and chairman of a White House task force on the American family, has been quoted as saying that his group's goal is "to tell children [that premarital sex] is wrong and explain why it's bad for them—not to teach them so much about sex that they can engage in it in early adolescence."

Moral Absolutes

The issue is not that sexual abstinence should not be recommended but, as sex-researchers Masters and Johnson have pointed out, that the recommendation is not always practical for all teen-agers. Not all teen-agers respond positively to moral absolutes, especially at a time when they are seeking to establish their independence. Most teens already know the traditional moral attitudes toward sex. What they do not understand as yet is the true

21

nature of sexual desire and how to give direction to that desire, which at their age is normal and natural. What is sometimes assumed by the profamily policies is that sex education and frank and open discussions of the facts of sexuality will contribute to increased teen-age sexual activity. In fact, the contrary is true.

A Canadian study of pregnant teen-agers found that these girls were so fearful of sex that they had avoided learning about sexual behavior and family planning. In fact, most of them never expected to have sexual intercourse. They were not without morals; but sex was something they could not really talk about or face honestly. One may conclude from this study that moral prohibitions do not ensure sexual abstinence and may only reinforce teenagers' urge to act out their sexual desires.

The belief that young people will learn from their mistakes seems also to be a myth. Several studies of young unmarried mothers have found that between 20 and 25 per cent became pregnant again within two years (with the rate going much higher among certain minority groups). The repeat of pregnancy appears to be related to a lack of knowledge about the risks of sexual intercourse, limited opportunity for further education, boredom with homelife, and the unavailability of a strong female support group.

Although peer pressures are especially great at this age, youth generally act out what they perceive to be adult values. Studies have found that young people's values are more continuous with those held by the important adults in their lives than is generally believed. To be effective, moral programs of education need to be consistent with the actual practices and attitudes of the larger society, and to be constant with the behavior of the adults that young people emulate. . . .

Maturity and Mobility

The number of teen-agers who are sexually active probably has not changed significantly in recent years, although some studies indicate that the age of sexual initiation may be dropping, possibly to as low as 13 or 14. This earlier age of initiation is due to several factors, including earlier physical maturation and greater mobility. A study by the Alan Guttmacher Institute found that American teen-agers are no more sexually active than young people in other Western countries, although the rate of pregnancy in the U.S. is significantly higher. The difference is that other societies often seem to hold more positive views of sex, to provide guidance in family planning and to offer comprehensive programs of sex education. The report concludes that the major focus in these other nations is not on morality but on finding constructive solutions to "prevent teen-age pregnancy and childbearing."

"Social attitudes toward the sexuality of young people become particularly important during adolescence."

Social Attitudes Affect Teenage Sexuality

Catherine S. Chilman

Catherine S. Chilman is a professor of social welfare at the University of Wisconsin-Milwaukee and the author of several books on adolescents. Chilman believes that sexuality is influenced by societal and cultural values. In the following viewpoint, Chilman writes that one's social status and cultural setting largely determine one's sexual mores. Chilman believes the social upheaval of the 1960s had a great impact on how society views teenage sexuality.

As you read, consider the following questions:

1. According to the author, why do sexual values differ between various social groups?
2. Why does Chilman believe one's culture is so influential during adolescence?
3. In the author's opinion, how did the 1960s alter sexual attitudes?

From *Adolescent Sexuality in a Changing American Society* by Catherine S. Chilman. Copyright © 1983 by John Wiley & Sons. Reprinted by permission of John Wiley & Sons Inc.

Social attitudes toward the sexuality of young people become particularly important during adolescence. Until recently, concepts of sex as sinful and as a dangerous primitive drive that had to be kept under strict control (especially for girls) created large problems of repression, denial, anxiety, and secrecy for both young people and the persons considered responsible for them (parents, human service professionals, and religious leaders). These concepts still exist but are countered by others that see sex as healthy, natural, and relatively safe (now that contraceptives and abortions are available).

The late 1960s and the 1970s witnessed radical upheavals in the culture of sexuality. Sex-specific attitudes and behaviors became highly permissive, and the push for equal sex roles at home and abroad became strong and widespread. In a sexually open and stimulating climate, young people as well as older ones were almost forced to take a fairly public stand regarding their sexual identity. This was especially difficult for teenagers because of their incomplete and vulnerable stage of psychosocial sexual development. In general, the absence of clear sexual guidelines provided both freedom and confused anxiety. The culture of sexuality differed somewhat in various regions of the country and for people of differing socioeconomic status.

Social Status

The extent to which social status makes a difference to the person depends on the degree of social stratification in a society and its meaning to that society. Although American society is less stratified than most and earlier definitions of social class have wavered under the impact of recent socioeconomic upheavals in this country, social status still makes a difference in the person's total development and current life situation. The effects of social status are also mediated by race, ethnicity, religion, and regional origins. All these demographic characteristics tend to affect cultural values—values that influence the way people view themselves and are viewed by others.

Culture evolves from the life history and experiences of a group and constitutes the group's attempt (over the years) to adapt to its environment. Culture plays an important part in the way the child is reared, from birth through adolescence and youth. The values, norms, beliefs, and expectancies of a group are intricately woven into all aspects of the developing person. They constitute many of the roots of personality, and it is both difficult and sometimes dangerous to try to change them.

Cultural Influences

Culture affects all aspects of sexuality; attitudes and behaviors concerning gender and sex identities, sexual expression, sex roles, mating, fertility control, and parenthood. Culture is most readily changed when the person's basic life situation is changed; when cultural leaders, with whom the individual can identify and wishes to identify, lead the way to new values and beliefs; and when the tools for change are made available.

There is considerable disagreement, at present, as to how much difference social status makes in contemporary American society. Class lines and values are not nearly so sharply defined as they were in earlier generations. The whole culture experienced such an upheaval in the 1960s that the country is witnessing pervasive "cultural confusion." The mass media (especially television) reach such an extensive audience that new ideas and beliefs are diffused much more rapidly than they formerly were.

Crumbling Social Structures

Why was it that teenagers became more sexually active in the 60s? I think anyone with an elementary sense of human psychology and anyone who can remember when he was a teenager can answer that question. When people my age and older were in high school we had hormonal drives and all of that stuff, but we also had a social structure that helped us maintain chastity. . . .

So what happened when they claimed that contraception and abortion were the answer to teenage pregnancy is that teenagers came under considerable pressure to become sexually active.

Michael Schwartz, *CCL News*, January-February 1987.

However, the life situation for the various social class and racial groups in the United States has not changed as much as some suppose and as many desire. The distribution of national income for individuals and families has not changed for at least 25 years. About 15 percent or more of the population still lives in poverty. Although the median income of American families has risen, the cost of living has outpaced these increases for most people in recent years. A small number of minority-group people have experienced marked improvements in income, educational opportunities, and employment, but the majority still suffers disproportionately from poverty, unemployment, underemployment, and, in general, access to "the good life."

Social Subgroups

The social status of adolescents is largely determined by the educational, occupational, and income characteristics of their parents. Those who come from families near the top of the socioeconomic ladder are apt to view themselves and their world in relatively optimistic, positive terms. In times of social change, such families tend to be cultural innovators because they have a basic security that allows them the freedom to be nontraditional. This often applies to their sexual attitudes and behaviors as well as other aspects of their lives.

Persons near the middle of the socioeconomic structure (including white-collar workers and upwardly mobile skilled laborers) are often beset by anxieties about losing the security they have and about failing to achieve the upward mobility to which so many of them aspire. Less secure than those at higher levels and more hopeful than those at lower ones, they tend to be more conventional and conservative because they have so much that may be gained—and so much that may be lost. In the area of sexuality, for example, this middle group tends to be more cautious and traditional with respect to sexual freedoms and contraceptive risk taking than those either at the top of the social heap or near or at the bottom.

Members of the less upwardly mobile blue-collar class and those in the lowest socioeconomic group are often alienated from society and its norms. Feeling little hope for the future and viewing society as essentially hostile and dangerous and themselves as powerless, they tend to react to the situation of the moment and take risks because they find life basically uncontrollable anyway.

Sex Roles

The culture largely determines how people are socialized for masculine and feminine sex roles. An enormous literature has developed on this topic in recent years. Sociologists have emphasized particularly the part played by socialization for sex roles in dating, marriage, family formation, and the like. For instance, if females are socialized to believe that their major function is childbearing, child care, and homemaking, then, quite naturally, they tend to feel these are their major life functions and seek to fulfill them. On the other hand, socialization for work and community roles outside the home and for roles shared with men tends to promote the desire for no or few children. In a similar vein, socialization of males that emphasizes their functions as father-providers or, in contrast, as role-sharing partners with employed women has a pronounced effect on the male's view of his life functions and goals.

Role socialization also affects attitudes toward sexual behaviors. Traditionally, more sexual freedom has been allowed to adolescent males because of the double standard of sex morality. This standard holds that males are "naturally sexy" and will "take what they can get." It is up to females to control the situation. There are two kinds of women: those who retain their virginity before marriage and are therefore pure, good, and lovable; and those who have premarital intercourse and are therefore to be sexually exploited, but neither loved nor married. Although these attitudes are changing, they are still prevalent, especially among blue-collar and lower-middle-class groups.

Role socialization varies by social class, religion, ethnicity, and race. In line with earlier comments, adolescents in the higher social classes are more likely to be socialized in nontraditional ways for fairly equal roles and freedoms between the sexes and for considerable sharing of interests and functions, both within and outside the home. Blue-collar youth, more traditional in their early socialization, are changing rapidly in their expressed attitudes toward more equalitarian sex roles. On the other hand . . . expressed attitudes are one thing, but the attempt to change enough to *live* these attitudes and to accept them emotionally is quite another. . . .

Social Acceptance

Without question, the sexual revolution and the women's and gay liberation movements have been instrumental in bringing into question some basic tenets of established theory and practice. Many aspects of sexual behavior formerly considered deviant have become the norm, with premarital intercourse for young people of both sexes and extramarital joint living arrangements almost commonplace. These changes have coincided with the growth of equality in sex roles, employment for women, and postponed marriage and family.

Zira DeFries, *Sexuality: New Perspectives*, 1985.

There is growing recognition that life situations and cultural climates can vary enormously for adolescents at different periods of history. For instance, youngsters who entered puberty in the radicalized 1960s were part of a huge population cohort that crowded the schools, created an enormous youth market and a strident youth culture, and, to a large extent, provided further fuel for the liberals in their revolt against all forms of authority, including the military. This is but one example of "times making (or helping to make) the teens." Impressive work by social scientists who are studying periods of social history and the effects of these periods on life course development are providing a broadened perspective of human attitudes and behaviors in the context of the total environment at various periods of time.

"There is no question . . . that teens learn about sexuality from the media."

The Media Affect Teenage Sexuality

Debra W. Haffner and Marcy Kelly

According to the Nielson and Radio Advisory Board reports, teenagers spend more time being entertained by the media than doing anything else except sleeping. In the following viewpoint, Debra W. Haffner and Marcy Kelly, researchers at the Center for Population Options, write that teenagers gain much of their sexual information from the media. Rather than allowing adolescents to passively consume media portrayals of sex, Haffner and Kelly believe that parents and educators should use the media to positively influence teens' sexual values.

As you read, consider the following questions:

1. What proof do the authors give that the media's role in sex education is not new?
2. According to Haffner and Kelly, how has television's portrayal of sex changed since 1985?
3. What is being done to improve the media's handling of sexual topics?

Excerpted from "Adolescent Sexuality in the Media" by Debra W. Haffner and Marcy Kelly, *SIECUS Report*, March/April 1987, pp. 9-11. Copyright © Sex Information and Education Council of the U.S. Reprinted by permission.

Papa don't preach, I'm in trouble deep.
Papa don't preach, I've been losing sleep.
But I made up my mind, I'm keeping my baby.
(Sire Records © 1986)

Let's take love step by step,
Let's go step by step,
Wait.
(Fuentes y Fomento Intercontinentales © 1985)

Two "number one" songs. The first, by Madonna, glorifies teenage childbearing. The second, by Tatiana and Johnny, is a hit in Mexico and Latin America that encourages young people to wait to have sexual intercourse. The second song, "Detente," has increased the number of young people in Mexico seeking information at family planning clinics. Will "Papa Don't Preach" affect American teenagers' behavior?

Did the increase in the number of explicit sexual references in teen-oriented music, television, and movies help lead to the increase in teen sexual activity, or does the portrayal of sex in the media reflect the changes American society has experienced in the last two decades? Sexuality educators share an uneasy alliance with radically conservative groups in our concern about what our children are learning about sex from the media. Most people agree with the report of the National Academy of Sciences that the media provides "young people with lots of clues about how to be sexy, but . . . little information about how to be sexually responsible."

Media's Role in Sexuality

The media plays a pervasive role in most Americans' lives. The average American family has a television set turned on over seven hours a day. Teenagers watch approximately 24 hours of television and listen to the radio an average of 18.5 hours a week. If one adds movies, teenagers are spending more time being entertained by the media than any other activity, with the possible exception of sleeping! . . .

The media has always provided sexuality information. The first radio soap operas airing in the 1930's focused on such issues as marriage, divorce, infidelity, and standards of correct behavior for men and women. Teen-oriented music, such as "Louis Louis" in the 1950's, the "House of the Rising Sun" in the 1960's and "Dancing in the Sheets" in the 1980's has titillated teens with its sexual messages while causing their parents to protest.

Television, radio, movies, and advertisements all play a role in our sexuality education. Sexuality in the media not only includes suggestive behaviors, but information about sex roles, family life, physical attractiveness, friendship, parent-child communication, pregnancy, and childbearing. The TV show *Moonlighting* not only includes frequent sexual innuendos, but provides messages about body image, male-female friendships, and working relationships and roles. *The Cosby Show* teaches us about family relationships, and in some ways, presents as difficult an idealized model as *Father Knows Best* and *The Brady Bunch*. Advertisements use highly attractive people in suggestive postures to encourage buying products that will somehow make us more sexually desirable. Music videos frequently feature sexual situations, sexist images, and sexual violence.

More Explicit

The media *has* become more explicit about sexual behaviors. In an analysis of specific sexual content in prime-time television, the investigators identified approximately 20,000 scenes of suggested sexual intercourse and behavior, sexual comments, and innuendos in one year of evening television. Sex on the afternoon soap operas is even more prevalent—and almost all sexual encounters on the soaps are between people who are not married to each other. During the late 1970's, there was a four-fold increase in flirtations and seductive behaviors on TV, a five-fold increase in the number of sexual innuendos, and almost a doubling of the number of implied acts of sexual intercourse. Verbal references to intercourse increased from 2 to 53 a week during this time.

Media Influence

The media is a pervasive force in all of our lives, but especially in the lives of children and adolescents. One can learn much about sexual behavior and attitudes condoned by society by looking at the Jordache jeans advertisements on television or in the New York Times Magazine section. Movies and other media sources are also providing clear messages about sexual behavior.

Andrea Parrot, *Human Sexuality*, 1984.

And yet, until very recently, contraception was considered a taboo subject for television entertainment programs. A famous *All in the Family* episode in the 1970's was about sterilization, and in *Maude*, Maude had an abortion. These were rare exceptions. In fact, a 1970's *James at 15* episode was never aired because the network refused to allow James to refer to contraception in a scene in which he was to lose his virginity. Indeed, until 1985, neither birth control in general, nor specific forms of contraception were mentioned on network television.

A major change has recently occurred. In 1985, generic terms like "birth control" and "contraception" became acceptable. This season [1986-87], actual methods of contraception are being discussed. For example, in "Babies Having Babies," a CBS daytime *School-Break Special*, the words, "rubber," "condom," and "birth

30

control'' were used. In NBC's *St. Elsewhere*, the terms ''IUD,'' ''condoms,'' and ''the pill'' were used this season, and ABC's *Choices* included mention of a ''diaphragm'' and ''birth control pills.''

Further, several shows have included honest portrayals of adolescent sexuality. In *Kate and Allie*, Allie counsels her daughter Jenny to postpone sexual intercourse, but to seek contraception if she doesn't wait. Harvey and Mary Beth Lacey of *Cagney and Lacey* counsel 16-year-old Harv, Jr. about condoms and educate early adolescent Michael about pornography. On *Fame, Mr. Belvedere, Facts of Life,* and *Growing Pains*, middle adolescent girls and boys have faced the decision to have first intercourse, and all have chosen abstinence. On the soap opera *Days of Our Lives*, a teenage couple chooses to have sex, and in groundbreaking episodes, visit a clinic and a drugstore for contraception.

Media Impact

There is considerable disagreement about whether the media influences us to change our attitudes and behaviors or whether it merely mirrors the changes in our society. There has been only limited research on the impact of media messages on teen sexual behavior, and what exists has offered conflicting results.

A 1981 study indicated that there was no link between the amount of television teens watched and the likelihood that they would have intercourse. However, another study found a strong correlation between the amount of sexually-oriented television watched, as a proportion of all TV viewed, and the probability that an adolescent had had intercourse. In another survey, researchers found that a preference for MTV and other music television programs was associated with increased sexual experience among middle adolescents, but not among early and late teens.

There is no question, however, that teens learn about sexuality from the media. Teens report that TV is equally or more encouraging about sexual intercourse than their friends, and high television use has been correlated with dissatisfaction about virginity among high school and college students. In fact students who think TV accurately portrays sex are more likely to be dissatisfied with their own first experiences.

Responsibility

The Center for Population Options has an office in Los Angeles that works with the entertainment media on portraying sexuality in a responsible manner. The three components of the program include a Media Advisory Service, a Media Awards Program, and a Seminars Series.

The Media Advisory Service assists media writers and producers with theme development, research, factual review, site visits,

31

TODAYS LESSON

SEX EDUCATION

ROTHCO

"WHY STUDY THAT STUFF IN SCHOOL?
WE GET IT ALL IN THE MAGS AND MOVIES."

shooting locales, script review, and consultation to improve the quality and increase the impact of sexual responsibility messages. The kinds of shows needing information range from dramatic and comedy series and Casey Kasem's "American Top 40" radio show to syndicated game shows and "Nightline."

As part of the Media Advisory Service, CPO has developed guidelines for the portrayal of sexuality in the media. These guidelines were developed by CPO's Media Advisory Committee, consisting of representatives from such major entertainment organizations as the Writers' Guild, Women in Film, the Academy of Television Arts and Sciences, NBC, Carson Productions, and Warner Brothers. The guidelines have been distributed nationwide to TV and film critics, members of the TV Academy, and network and production companies.

These guidelines offer the following suggestions for the presentation of responsible sexual content:

- Recognize sex as a healthy and natural part of life.
- Parent and child conversations about sex are important and healthy and should be encouraged.
- Demonstrate that not only the young, unmarried, and beautiful have sexual relationships.
- Not all affection and touching must culminate in sex.
- Portray couples having sexual relationships with feelings of affection, love, and respect for each other.
- Consequences of unprotected sex should be discussed or shown.
- Miscarriage should not be used as a dramatic convenience for resolving an unwanted pregnancy.
- Use of contraception should be indicated as a normal part of a sexual relationship.
- Avoid associating violence with sex or love.
- Rape should be depicted as a crime of violence, not one of passion.
- The ability to say "no" should be recognized and respected. . . .

A Tool for Sex Education

Sexuality educators can use the media to help children and adolescents learn about sexuality. David Green's excellent monograph, "Sex on TV: A Guide for Parents," encourages parents to develop active viewing skills in order to understand TV's role in sexuality education. He encourages parents to initiate conversations about sexual issues by discussing TV characters and their actions.

Sexuality educators can use the media to supplement lessons. Students can be asked to clip advertisements as a springboard for a discussion of standards of physical attractiveness and sex role stereotypes. Movies such as *Killing Us Softly* and *Stale Buns* can help sensitize students about the role that sex plays in advertising. Students can dissect the lyrics of popular songs to explore their sexual messages. Parents and children can be asked to discuss what their favorite shows tell them about sex roles, family life, intimacy, and communication. Parent seminars can focus on how to use the media to stimulate discussions about sexual topics.

"Sex is . . . being taught to youngsters through the wide distribution of pornography."

Pornography Affects Teenage Sexuality

Kenneth S. Kantzer

Though pornography is theoretically off-limits to teenagers under age 18, sexually-explicit books, magazines, and videos are easily accessible to American youth. What effect does this material have on teenage sexuality? In the following viewpoint, Kenneth S. Kantzer argues that pornography gives teens a perverted perspective on sexuality. Kantzer, a writer for the evangelical Christian magazine *Christianity Today*, writes that the main consumers of pornography are 15- to 19-year-old males. The author believes that parents, educators, and church leaders should teach teenagers positive sexual values to counter the negative influence of pornography.

As you read, consider the following questions:

1. According to Kantzer, what lessons do teens learn from pornography?
2. What suggestions does the author make to combat pornography's negative influence?
3. In Kantzer's opinion, what myth about pornography must be overcome?

Kenneth S. Kantzer, "The Real Sex Ed Battle," *Christianity Today*, April 17, 1987. Copyright 1987 by CHRISTIANITY TODAY. Used by permission.

In all the furor over whether sex ought to be taught in the public schools, one fact is often overlooked: Sex is *already* being taught to youngsters through the wide distribution of pornography. And recent findings on the effects of pornography on the young ought to mobilize an even greater ground swell of public outrage aimed at publishers of pornography.

Since 1970, pornographers have enjoyed the support of a U.S. presidential commission report downplaying the effects of pornography. That report "found no evidence to date that exposure to explicit sexual materials plays a significant role in the causation of delinquent or criminal behavior." Rather, it presented pornographic material as essentially harmless entertainment that often had a cathartic influence upon those who used it. But [in] July [1986] the U.S. Department of Justice issued a two-volume report that reverses those findings.

Harmful Influence

The Justice Department's report comes at a time when research has called into question most of the basic conclusions of the 1970 commission. Specifically, it raises questions about the "cathartic" theory espoused by the older report. Experimentation with pornography does not always lead to satiation and boredom (thus serving as a harmless fantasy outlet for those who would otherwise engage in rape or other forms of sexual abuse, so the theory goes). Quite to the contrary, viewing some kinds of hard-core pornography tends to foster imitation. The 1986 report notes that research "shows a causal relationship between exposure to material of this type and aggressive behavior towards women." Rapists interviewed in prison were 15 times more likely than nonoffenders to have been exposed to hard-core pornography during the ages of 6 to 10.

Here we are not dealing with so-called adult entertainment. Rather, we are confronted with the favorable treatment of criminal acts against children and women. What is most alarming is that this offensive material may be the most prevalent form of sex education for our nation's youth. According to Henry Boatwright, chairman of the U.S. Advisory Board for Social Concerns, 70 percent of all pornographic magazines end up in the hands of minors. One member of the commission estimated that the chief consumers of even hard-core pornography are males 15 to 19 years old.

And what lessons do young people assimilate from such instruction? The movies, magazines, and books teach these impressionable youth that women are playthings, that sex has little to do with love and need not be tied to commitment or fidelity, and that sexual activity is appropriate anywhere, with anyone, and at any time.

35

No wonder the number of unmarried couples living together has quadrupled; abortions among unmarried women more than doubled (500,000 to over 1,200,000 per year); and single-parent families tripled (1,900,000 to 5,600,000). Meanwhile, teenage pregnancy in the U.S. is the highest in the world—over one million each year with more than half ending in abortion.

Though Christians have admirably joined the battle to prevent the wide distribution of pornography, more must be done to combat this calculated effort to educate our youth. Few understand just how serious the purveyors of pornography are in making their message available. The Playboy Foundation, for example, underwrote the formation of the Organization for Free Press to counter efforts against the distribution of pornography. And the public relations firm of Gray and Company proposed to members of a media coalition a $900,000 annual budget to fight the strong opposition that has risen against pornography. The underlying strategy of such efforts is to portray those who oppose pornography as narrow-minded religious bigots, ultraconservative in their attitudes toward life, hopelessly outdated, and determined to destroy freedom of speech and freedom of press in all other areas of American life.

Pornography

It has become increasingly clear to us that many children who escape actual sexual abuse are nevertheless receiving their primary education in human sexuality from a graphically inappropriate source. Such a source describes sexual fulfillment as conditioned upon transience, dominance, aggression, or degradation.

Bruce Ritter, *The Wanderer*, July 24, 1986.

What do we recommend? The first line of defense against pornography's vile influence is to instruct our children in a sound and healthful view of sex. This is no time to retreat behind a false sense of biblical modesty. We must take for granted that our children will be bombarded with a hedonistic philosophy of sex, not only from publications recognized as pornographic, but from the flood of material that comes to them incessantly through public advertising, radio, and television (including the "family programs" run at the prime hours of the day). It is far better that our children receive their sex education within the framework of a biblical philosophy of sex as an honorable and treasured gift of God. The Christian home, Christian schools, Sunday schools, church youth groups, seminars, and youth retreats—these are the appropriate places for instructing our children about sex.

Second, we must speak out boldly in our neighborhoods, at

parent-teacher meetings, and at local newsstands, drugstores, and bookstores. This is an issue on which evangelicals really do have a moral majority. A 1985 Gallup Poll showed that 73 percent of the American people believed explicit sexual magazines and movies influence some people to commit rape or other sexual violence. And 93 percent called for stricter control of magazines displaying sexual violence. We must take the lead in speaking out boldly and fearlessly against this festering sore in our society.

Third, we must be willing to back others who take a stand, joining them in petition drives and boycotts in the fight against stores that display or sell pornographic materials and against television programs that carry debasing sexual themes.

A Need for Education

Fourth, we must support studies so that our opposition is based on a clear understanding of the difference between opposition to pornography and opposition to freedom of speech. This, after all, is the final defense of most proponents of pornography. They warn that any laws that bar obscenity will inevitably lead to laws destroying our constitutional freedoms of press and speech. We can combat this defense by educating ourselves (and the public) regarding definitions of pornography and obscenity.

For too long, the public has accepted the myth that pornography harms no one, even the legions of minors who are frequently exposed to it. The Justice report effectively dashes that notion. If the church cares to enter the real sex-education battle, it would be wise to step up the attack on easy-to-obtain smut and accept responsibility for the sex education of our youth.

Recognizing Statements That Are Provable

From various sources of information we are constantly confronted with statements and generalizations about social and moral problems. In order to think clearly about these problems, it is useful if one can make a basic distinction between statements for which evidence can be found and other statements which cannot be verified or proved because evidence is not available, or the issue is so controversial that it cannot be definitely proved.

Readers should constantly be aware that magazines, newspapers, and other sources often contain statements of a controversial nature. The following activity is designed to allow experimentation with statements that are provable and those that are not.

The following statements are taken from the viewpoints in this chapter. Consider each statement carefully. *Mark P for any statement you believe is provable. Mark U for any statement you feel is unprovable because of the lack of evidence. Mark C for any statements you think are too controversial to be proved to everyone's satisfaction.*

If you are doing this activity as a member of a class or group, compare your answers with those of other class or group members. Be able to defend your answers. You may discover that others will come to different conclusions than you. Listening to the reasons others present for their answers may give you valuable insights in recognizing statements that are provable.

P = *provable*
U = *unprovable*
C = *too controversial*

38

1. Culture affects all aspects of sexuality: sex roles, sexual expression, mating, and parenthood.

2. Television, radio, movies, and advertisements play a primary role in our sexuality education.

3. Adolescent males are allowed more sexual freedom because of the double standard concerning sexual morality.

4. Culture largely determines how people are socialized into masculine and feminine sex roles.

5. Adolescents in high social classes are more likely to establish equal sex roles between the sexes.

6. The cornerstone of sexual maturity is the ability to care unselfishly for someone else.

7. Christian homes, churches, and youth groups are the appropriate places for instructing teenagers about sex.

8. The media has become more explicit about sexual behavior.

9. Schools and peers contribute to the process of sexual maturation.

10. The adult sexual attitudes of American youth emerge by the senior year of high school.

11. There is intense peer pressure on girls to "go all the way."

12. Healthy social-sexual behavior results from the influence of family, peers, and schools.

13. The chief consumers of hard-core pornography are males 15 to 19 years old.

14. It is far better that children receive their sex education within the framework of biblical philosophy than through pornography.

15. The media simply mirror the changes in sexual attitudes within US society.

16. There is a relationship between exposure to pornography and aggressive behavior toward women.

17. During the late 1970s there was a five-fold increase in the number of sexual innuendos on television.

Periodical Bibliography

The following articles have been selected to supplement the diverse views presented in this chapter.

Stephanie Kilby Auerbach, Betsey Nathan, Donna O'Hare, and Milagros Benedicto — "Impact of Ethnicity," *Society*, November/December 1985.

Vincent Bozzi — "Teens of a Feather," *Psychology Today*, April 1986.

Anne Husted Burleigh — "*Seventeen* Loses Its Innocence," *Catholicism in Crisis*, February 1986.

Allan C. Carlson — "Pregnant Teenagers and Moral Civil War," *Human Life Review*, Fall 1985.

Sarah Crichton — "Off the Beach Blanket and into the Bedroom," *Ms.*, June 1985.

John Deedy — "Are Kids Being Seduced by a Turned-On World?" *U.S. Catholic*, May 1985.

Kathy McCoy — "How Your Parents' Values About Sex Affect You," *Seventeen*, April 1984.

Sue Mittenthal — "New Sexual Attitudes," *Glamour*, September 1985.

Richard John Neuhaus — "Policy by Pathology," *National Review*, December 5, 1986.

Mary O'Connell — "How To Take the Romance Out of Sex," *SALT*, April 1987.

Elizabeth Stark — "Young, Innocent and Pregnant," *Psychology Today*, October 1986.

U.S. News & World Report — "Mothers Raising Mothers," March 17, 1986.

What Kind of Sex Education Is Appropriate for Teenagers?

Chapter Preface

According to many health-care providers, teenagers are in dire need of quality education about sexual matters. However, parents, educators, and religious leaders disagree over the questions of who should be responsible for sex education and what should be taught.

Some argue that school-based sex education courses heighten students' curiosity and lead to greater sexual experimentation. They believe sex education curricula should promote moral values concerning premarital sex. Other critics go even further and maintain that sex education should not be addressed in schools, but be taught at home where family values can be promoted.

Supporters of sex education programs agree that, ideally, sexual information should be obtained at home. But parents are often ill-informed or reluctant to talk with their children about sex. For this reason, it is important that all high school and junior high students receive accurate information concerning reproduction and birth control at school.

This issue remains controversial because of the moral, religious, and philosophical factors involved. The authors in the following chapter present their versions of the best solution to this divisive topic.

"We owe it to our children and their children to provide them with the [sexual] information they need."

Sex Education
Is Necessary

Sol Gordon

Sex education in public schools has remained a controversial issue for over two decades. Critics of sex education argue that teaching students about sex causes them to experiment, while supporters counter that information about reproduction is necessary to combat unwanted pregnancy and sexually-transmitted diseases. The following viewpoint is written by psychologist Sol Gordon, professor emeritus at Syracuse University and a well-known expert on sex education. In it, he argues that quality sex education is necessary for today's teens. Gordon maintains that knowledge is superior to ignorance when dealing with teenage sexuality.

As you read, consider the following questions:

1. According to Gordon, why does the US have a high rate of teenage pregnancy?
2. Why does the author write that parents and the media are ineffective sex educators?
3. What types of questions does Gordon think sex education should address?

Sol Gordon, "What Kids Need To Know," *Psychology Today*, October 1986. Reprinted with permission from PSYCHOLOGY TODAY Magazine. Copyright © 1986 American Psychological Association.

If you tell kids about sex, they'll do it. If you tell them about VD, they'll go out and get it. Incredible as it may seem, most opposition to sex education in this country is based on the assumption that knowledge is harmful. But research in this area reveals that ignorance and unresolved curiosity, not knowledge, are harmful.

Our failure to tell children what they want and need to know is one reason we have the highest rates of out-of-wedlock teen pregnancy and abortion of any highly developed country in the world. And we pay a big price monetarily and otherwise in dealing with the more than one million teenage pregnancies every year, as well as several million new cases of sexually transmitted diseases.

A Solution

Poor education, of course, is only one cause of teenage pregnancy. Such factors as poverty, racism and sexism are even more crucial. But there is ample evidence to show that relevant sex education is part of the solution to teenage pregnancy.

At the Institute for Family Research and Education at Syracuse University, we have been studying questions related to sex education for more than 15 years. Some people still seem to think they can and should be the only sex educators of their children. My response is, "How can that be? You'll have to wrap your children in cotton and not allow them to leave their bedrooms, watch TV or read newspapers or current magazines. You certainly can't allow them to have any friends or go to any public school bathroom."

The idea that kids get information about sex from their parents is completely erroneous. Even the college-educated parents of my Syracuse University students offer very little. In survey after survey in a period of 12 years involving more than 8,000 students, fewer than 15 percent reported that they received a meaningful sex education from their parents. Usually girls were told about menstruation. The rest of the teaching could be summed up in one word: DON'T. The boys were on their own except for an occasional single prepuberty talk with Dad, who made vague analogies involving the birds and bees and ended the talk with "if worst comes to worst, be sure to use a rubber."

Poor Sex Education

One reason parents have for not educating their children is discomfort with their own sexual feelings and behavior. Part of this discomfort derives from the fact that they themselves received little or no sex education as children. Without one's parents to draw upon as a model, the cycle of noncommunication is repeated from generation to generation.

If parents don't do the job, do kids get their sex education through the media? Of course not. TV is full of antisexual messages

44

of rape, violence and infidelity. This is especially true of the soaps, watched by an increasingly large number of teenagers via delayed video recordings. When was the last time you saw a really good sex-education program on TV or an article in your local newspaper? There are a few exceptions to this sex-education wasteland. Teenagers who read, particularly girls, do get some good information from Judy Blume and her novels, such as *Forever* and *Are You There God? It's Me, Margaret*, and magazines such as *Teen* and *Seventeen*.

LEARNING THE HARD WAY

What about schools? Probably fewer than 10 percent of American schoolchildren are exposed to anything approaching a meaningful sex education. There are some good programs and some dedicated and well-trained teachers, but I doubt there are a dozen school districts that have a kindergarten through 12th-grade sex-education program that even approaches those available in Sweden. American teenagers typically score abysmally low on sex-knowledge questionnaires.

Sex education in the United States today, where it exists at all, is usually a course in plumbing—a relentless pursuit of the fallopian tubes. The lack of real education is obscured by the answers to surveys that ask students if they've had sex education in their schools. More than half respond, "Yes." What most surveys don't ask—or if they do, what doesn't get reported—are the really important questions such as:

(Q) How much sex education did you have?

(A) Two classes in menstruation for girls only in the sixth grade.

(Q)How effective was the education?

(A) I slept through it.

(Q) By whom was it taught?

(A) One gym teacher proclaimed to the boys, "Hey fellows, the thing between your legs is not a muscle—don't exercise it."

Useful sex education should tell children what they want and need to know. And we know what they want to know. At the Institute for Family Research and Education at Syracuse University, we have reviewed more than 50,000 questions teenagers from all over the country have submitted, anonymously, to us and to their teachers. Not one teenager has ever asked a question about fallopian tubes. Young people want to know about homosexuality, penis size, masturbation, female orgasm, and the answers to such questions as how can I tell if I'm really in love, what constitutes sexual desire, what is the best contraceptive, when are you most likely to get pregnant and various questions about oral and anal sex. Recently, the most frequent one seems to be why boys are only interested in girls for sex.

Proper Framework

Before I talk to teenagers about questions like these, I try to place the issue of sexuality in a proper framework. I tell kids that of the 10 most important aspects of a mature relationship, number one is love and commitment. Number two is a sense of humor. (I advise parents not to have teenagers unless they have a sense of humor.) Number three is meaningful communication. Sex is somewhere down on the list, just ahead of sharing household tasks together.

I also tell them that I, like most parents, don't think teenagers should engage in sexual intercourse. They are too young and too vulnerable. They aren't prepared to handle the fact that the first experiences of sex are usually grim. Almost no one will have an orgasm. The boy gets his three days later when he tells the guys about it.

Fewer than one in seven use a reliable form of contraception the first time they have sex. In contrast, the large majority of Swedish teenagers use contraception the very first time and consistently afterwards. But knowing that most teenagers will have sex before they finish high school, I say to them, if you are not going to listen to me (or your parents) about postponing sex, use contraception.

The simple message—No. Don't, Stop—doesn't work. The double message—No, But. . . . —is more effective. Look at how alcohol education is now being handled by many parents and school organizations. They say, "I don't think you should drink, but if you get carried away and you drink anyway, don't drive. Call me and we'll arrange alternate transportation." When it comes to premarital sex, a parent might start with "No" and try to convince the teenager to hold back but also provide the "But"—reliable contraceptive information. As the Talmud says, expect miracles but don't count on them. . . .

Other Questions

What else do we need to tell young people? Tell the boys not to worry about penis size. You can't tell the size of the penis by observing its detumescent state. (Freud got it wrong—men are the ones with penis envy.) Reassure girls about their vaginas—one size fits all.

A Right To Know

I believe that education about sexuality is information that students have a right and a need to know, just as they have a right and a need to know fractions or English grammar. If we approach sexuality education with this goal uppermost in mind (rather than viewing sexuality education as a political statement, as a way of solving the teenage pregnancy problem or as a way of gaining access to students for other services), we are forced to focus on creating programs that make it as easy as possible for teachers to present sensitive information accurately, and in a manner that enables students to learn, to retain knowledge and to apply what they've learned.

Lana D. Muraskin, *Family Planning Perspectives,* July/August 1986.

One or a few homosexual experiences or thoughts don't make a person homosexual. Homosexuals are people who in their adult lives are attracted to and have sexual relations with others of the same sex. The preference is not subject to conscious control. Sexual orientation is not a matter of choice. It's not OK to be antigay.

For teenagers, few questions are as urgent as: How can I tell if I'm really in love? I've probably listened to more nonsense in this area that any other. I've heard the same rubbish so many times that I've come up with some standard responses to the following:

Love is blind. I think love is blind for only 24 hours. Then you have to open your eyes and notice with whom you're in love.

Love at first sight. I advise people to take another look.

You can fall in love only once. This silly idea can have tragic results.

How many young Romeos and Juliets have committed suicide after the breakup of a torrid love affair, thinking that life is over for them? No, I tell them, you can fall in love at least 18 times.

Will I know when I'm really in love? Certainly. If you feel you are in love, you are. (Parents should never trivialize a teenager's love affair. However brief, it's always serious.) But I tell teenagers there are two kinds of love—mature love and immature. Mature lovers are energized. They want to please each other. They are nice to parents who are nice to them. Immature love is exhausting. Immature lovers are too tired to do their schoolwork. They are not nice to those they should care about—parents, siblings, even their dogs and cats.

The Need for Sex Education

Sex-education courses that cover even a few of these real concerns are being taught almost nowhere in this country. It's up to parents to make a start, whether they are comfortable with the subject or not. You don't have to be comfortable to educate your children. I daresay most of us are uncomfortable about a lot of things these days, but we keep doing our jobs anyway. We should at least teach teachers, psychologists, clergy, social workers and others who work with youngsters how to respond to young people's questions.

We owe it to our children and their children to provide them with the information they need in a manner they will accept. I sometimes use humor. It helps reduce anxiety and puts teenagers in a receptive mood. An old Zen expression says, "When the mind is ready a teacher appears."

"Today's sex education is one of the most devastating things that can possibly happen to any society."

Sex Education
Is Harmful

Melvin Anchell, interviewed by John F. McManus

The content of sex education programs has received careful scrutiny from concerned parents, educators, and religious leaders. Some of these people advocate keeping sex education out of the schools and implementing it in family homes where moral values can be taught. In the following viewpoint, Melvin Anchell, a retired psychiatrist, maintains that sex education in the schools harms students. Anchell, in an interview with journalist John F. McManus, argues that amoral sexual instruction needlessly confuses students and drives them to self-destructive behavior such as premarital sex, drug addiction, alcohol abuse, and suicide.

As you read, consider the following questions:

1. According to Anchell, how does sex education disrupt sexual development?
2. What is the main theme of sex education programs, in the author's opinion?
3. What is Anchell's suggestion for the future of sex education?

Q. *Dr. Anchell, you have been very critical of sex education courses. Please tell us why.*

A. From a physician's standpoint, today's sex education is one of the most devastating things that can possibly happen to any society, and it certainly has overwhelmed our society. For over one hundred years, established psychoanalytic precepts, which have repeatedly been substantiated by clinical observations, reveal two important facts concerning human sexuality. The first is that life-sustaining human sexual needs can only be fulfilled in an affectionate, monogamous, heterosexual relationship. In this type of relationship, the affectionate part plays as important a role as the physical part. Needless to say, sex educators do not stress this fact even though it is an extremely important aspect of human sexuality. For human sexuality to be complete, there must be a confluence, a union, of the affectionate and physical components of the human sexual instinct. When affectionate needs are weakened and physical sex is all that remains, sex becomes meaningless and life becomes empty.

Disrupting Sexual Adjustment

Q. *What is the other fact about human sexuality?*

A. The second salient psychoanalytic fact is that, in humans, unlike in any other creatures, three phases of sexual development occur before mature adult sexuality is reached. The public school courses given during each of these phases cause great harm to students and society in general.

Kindergarten through 12th grade sex education programs, sponsored throughout our nation by Planned Parenthood and related organizations such as the Alan Guttmacher Institute, severely disrupt natural sexual growth. The sex teachings rend apart natural sexual processes making it virtually impossible for a sexually indoctrinated student to make mature sexual adjustments.

Q. *What are the three phases of sexual development in humans?*

A. The first phase of sexual development begins at birth and lasts through the fifth year of life. The second phase occurs during the sixth through twelfth years. And the third phase starts at puberty, usually about age thirteen, and lasts until early adulthood. . . .

The Third Phase

Q. *Tell us what happens to youngsters in the third phase of sexual development.*

A. The last phase of human sexual development begins at approximately 13, and continues throughout adolescence and into early adulthood. In this final phase, direct sexual energies are once again reawakened and latency comes to an end. In the case of the thirteen-year-old and adolescent boys, the reawakened sexual energies are direct and are centered in the genitalia. The erotic feelings of pubescent and adolescent girls follow a much different course. Their sexual feelings may be as intense as those of a boy, but the eroticisms of the young female are not intertwined with the sex act as they are in the young male.

Wayward bus

John Knudsen, reprinted with permission.

Q. *Please explain how a normal young girl's sexuality will develop.*
A. Because a girl's genital structures have not been familiar to her all through her life as a boy's have to him, and because they are biologically unready and remain anesthetic to sexual intercourse until much later in life, and because her feminine and motherhood psychology is not completed until late adolescence, nature has provided the young female with a natural aversion to sexual intercourse. Normally, her erotic feelings are completely and healthfully expressed in sensual fantasies and dreams, the

51

wishes to love and be loved, words of love, kisses and caresses, and sometimes thoughts of having a child. Now these are natural inborn expressions of the adolescent female's sexual needs. But you would never know it by what is happening to our youngsters today.

The dichotomy between the adolescent boy's readiness for sex and the girl's natural inhibition to the sex act serves vital purposes. Nature always has reason for what it does. The young girl's natural reluctance should not be disturbed; it strengthens affectionate feelings and leads to the spiritualization of sex.

Building Tensions

Q. *How should sexuality properly develop? And what can be expected if normal progression is trampled upon?*

A. The spiritualization of sex and feelings of esteem for the sex partner are essential if the needs of the human sexual instinct are to be fulfilled. When affectionate and mental prerequisites are not met and physical sex is all that remains, frustrations result which eventually build up into tensions and depressions. For relief from these tensions and depressions, many sexually educated and sexually active pre-teen and teen youths turn to alcohol, drugs, perversions and, not infrequently, suicide.

When the life sustaining sexual instincts are perverted, the death instincts take over. This is one of nature's inexorable laws. Teen suicide now ranks as the second leading cause of death in young people under twenty-one.

Q. *How would you characterize sex education programs generally?*

A. There is one main theme in school sex education programs, and that theme is carnality. Today's sex education programs are "how to" courses that teach and condone fornication and all types of perverted sex acts. The sex education courses saturate students with an overtolerance for perverts. Such saturation and overtolerance destroy the normal, inborn defense mechanism to shun the pervert and thereby avoid contamination.

Today's K-through-12 sex education programs lead young people into becoming conscienceless, polymorphous sexual robots capable of engaging in any kind of sex act with indifference and without guilt. These are the characteristics of pimps and prostitutes.

Desensitizing Students

Q. *Does sex education induce a callousness toward life?*

A. Yes. Along with desensitizing the minds of students year after year with information about indiscriminate sex acts that are engaged in with indiscriminate partners, sex educators provide detailed information on contraception and abortion. The persuasiveness used to teach abortion has so desensitized students to abortion that, should a sexually educated girl become pregnant, she submits to having these psychologically mutilating operations with about as much concern as having a manicure.

Q. *Don't sex educators themselves see the harm they are doing?*

A. Sex educators have either a mental block—that is, a strong repression—or for some other reason cannot see that more than 20 years of K-through-12 sex education programs in America are directly responsible for the national sexual calamity that is rife among today's youth. The sex educators not only deny their own accountability but have the temerity to regard themselves as the saviors of young people. They even claim that they are protecting youngsters from false standards and values based on didactic family attitudes and anachronistic morals associated with out-moded religion.

At no time do the sex education teachers remotely suggest that the *cure* for today's teen and pre-teen pregnancies, abortions, pros-titutions, perversions, criminalities, and psychological as well as physical venereal diseases necessitates that the educational system uphold the family and the basics of Judeo-Christian morality. They have no interest in a morality that supports the struggle for ex-istence, that seeks to save civilized life.

Immoral Influence

The basic idea behind sex education is that good information leads to good behavior. But good behavior, especially in an area like sex, toward which all have a strong inclination, results from moral imperatives.

Can the government schools supply any moral perspective? Everyone knows that they cannot. Teachers are forbidden to counsel youngsters that premarital or extramarital intercourse is wrong, that homosexual practices violate nature, and that sexuality is part of the Almighty's plan for propagating the human race.

As a result, school-based sex-ed courses can't help but trample all over religious strictures. As has already been shown, they countenance abortion and contraception (which are repugnant to many), drive a wedge between numerous parents and their children, and expose youngsters to attitudes and practices relative to AIDS that most will find disgusting but some will find titillating.

John F. McManus, *The New American*, January 19, 1987.

Q. *What do you think of Surgeon General Koop's recommendation that sex education courses, including instruction about homosexuality and AIDS, begin at the third grade?*

A. This man must be completely void of psychological knowledge concerning human sexuality. I could not disagree more with his recommendation.

Q. *How do individuals become homosexual?*

A. Sex educators are trying to promulgate the idea that homosexuality is something one is born with—an inherited disposition. For over one hundred years of psychoanalytic investigation, it has been shown that, if you analyze even the 100 percent homosexual—that is, a person who engages in sexual activity only with members of his own sex—you will find that some childhood sexual impression or seduction invariably created that condition. As far as I am concerned, and I am aware that some doctors may not agree with me, my clinical observations and those of a vast number of other physicians show that homosexuality is not inherited. The condition is strictly due to some sort of seduction that occurred to these individuals in early childhood.

Homosexuality has also become very prevalent in our society today because our society fails to put any restraints on these people and has legalized their sex aims—sodomy, oral and anal sexual practices, etc. When society does not disavow such perversity, but instead begins to glorify these people and their sexual vulgarity, their ranks grow. We find this in savage and primitive communities, too. Where there is no stigma attached to homosexual activity, homosexuals form a large part of the population. This phenomenon also characterizes a civilization that is in decline.

Q. *Do you feel that there will be a cure for AIDS?*

A. I sincerely hope that a way can be found to cure AIDS. But I must tell you, as a physician, that it is the worst disease I have seen in 40 years of medical practice. It results from a virus that mutates very easily and is, therefore, going to be very difficult to capture. The flu virus is similar in that it tends to change its characteristics very quickly. At about the time a person is given a flu shot to prevent the disease in the coming year, a mutation may have occurred so that he or she is not protected. The AIDS virus is going to be an extremely difficult bug to stop. While I hope there is some answer, I doubt it will be forthcoming soon.

Remove Sex Education

Q. *What do you recommend instead of sex education?*

A. For the continued existence of a civilization composed of individuals living by conscience instead of a civilization made up of barbarians living by instinct only, the sexually gangrenous material filling the minds of our children and young people as a result of today's sex education courses and the pornographic entertainment media must be removed.

A tourniquet preventing the further spread of these contaminations is sorely needed. Sexual decency and life-sustaining, affectionate, monogamous heterosexuality must be maintained, not only in the home, but also in the schools to which we send our children.

> *"If we as parents do not teach our children about sex, they will probably gain information from the wrong source."*

Sex Education Belongs in the Home

Tim LaHaye

The diversity of American values makes sex education a controversial subject. Who can best teach America's youth about sex? Tim LaHaye, the president of Family Life Services and author of several books on sex and marriage, believes parents must teach their children their own sexual values. In the following viewpoint, LaHaye argues that schools cannot be allowed to indoctrinate students in "secular humanist" ideas of sexuality that conflict with Christian family values.

As you read, consider the following questions:

1. According to the author, why is it imperative that children receive sex education at an early age?
2. Why does LaHaye write that schools cannot be trusted to teach sex education?
3. In LaHaye's opinion, what is the parents' role in sex education?

We may be as certain as death and taxes that someone is going to teach our children about sex. It could be the dirty little kid down the street who knows everything that is wrong and ugly. It may be the cable TV program that's turned on some night when we're not home. Or possibly a secular humanist evangelist of sex education in the public school who does not share our moral values and will serve as a self-appointed guru of sexuality. It may even be a child molester. If we as parents do not teach our children about sex, they will probably gain information from the wrong source.

Sex is the most difficult subject in the world to discuss, and most people either avoid it or inject humor into the conversation, lowering the discussion to an unsavory level or reducing its significance. In most cases, parents—even good parents who responsibly teach their children about everything else they should know—somehow tend to avoid the issue of sex altogether.

Sex is such an intimate subject that it usually produces a strong emotional reaction, depending on a person's background. If you were not introduced to it casually and respectfully by your parents, you will probably find it difficult to discuss objectively. But you can learn to treat it like other significant matters and incorporate it into the training of your children. If it is "embarrassing" or "difficult" and you ignore it as so many parents do, your decision may be fatal to your children—or it may cause them to enter marriage already pregnant or emotionally and mentally crippled.

Self-Defense

In the history of the world, it has never been more imperative that children gain information about sex at an early age. No matter how much we try, we cannot prevent even young children from learning about the subject long before they need to. Thus the sex education of children by their parents becomes a matter of self-defense. We can only be sure our children learn the essential facts together with moral values if we serve as the instructors ourselves. We must not leave this vital task to others, for in so doing we risk leaving our children vulnerable to sexual exploitation. In fact, we should assume in this sex-crazed day that our children will eventually be confronted with sexual temptation. The only safeguard is parental preparation for that day. Most exploitation of children could be avoided by mental and moral training.

Parents may fail to teach their children about sex because they do not feel qualified. One mother asked, "Who am I to teach my child about sex?" I answered, "Her parent!" That is our primary qualification. This sincere mother clearly wanted the best for her daughter, but she made a common mistake. She thought that comprehensive knowledge about sexuality was the major requirement for being her child's educator. She did not understand that a little

"What's the matter with you, Perkins? Don't you want to grow up a fit member of the adult society?"

research . . . could make up for her deficiencies while still safeguarding the central point of sex education—teaching moral values.

One of the time-honored rights of parents in this country is teaching moral values to their children. Some in education and government, however, consider it *their* right; thus they are doing everything in their power to impose amorality on children. Surrender of our parental rights will guarantee the loss of our children, who are our most important possession. . . .

For more than 175 years, American public schools included few or no formal sex education classes. If the subject was taught at all, it appeared in conjunction with physical education or biology. Now, however, many schools offer two-or-three-week sessions every year for twelve years. Having lectured hundreds of times on the subject and having written a best-selling book on sexual adjustment in marriage, I believe we can teach most people all the basic ingredients in two or three hours just prior to marriage. One hour of instruction a day, five days a week, for three weeks a year times twelve years equals 180 hours. That is not education; it amounts to indoctrination of young people that easily leads to an obsession. But the amount of time devoted to this in the classroom is not my only objection to sex education in public schools.

The secular humanists who control SIECUS [Sex Information and Education Council of the United States] and Planned Parenthood (organizations that frequently provide lecturers for schools) and a large percentage of the curriculum designers are evolutionists. Many are also atheists. Why is that important? Because an atheistic evolutionist considers man an animal that does not possess an innate conscience and is not responsible to God for his behavior. He rejects moral absolutes, insisting that each generation establish its own judgments of right and wrong. In fact, modern education repeatedly affirms that "there are no rights and wrongs." Nowhere is that false notion more harmful than in the sex-education classroom. . . .

Teach Moral Values

Teaching sex education in mixed classes to hot-blooded teenagers without benefit of moral values is like pouring gasoline on emotional fires. An explosion is inevitable.

The enjoyment of sexual relations is and, for morally minded people, always has been an adult experience. Furthermore, our culture has consistently taught that individuals should not engage in intercourse until the participants are willing to take responsibility for their actions—in other words, become parents. Sexual activity will eventually lead to parenthood, as any of the more than one million pregnant, unwed school girls in America each year will testify. Who authorized these self-styled "sexologists" to teach our children otherwise? Who elected them to change our centuries-old tradition that left sexual matters in the domain of the family? Who commissioned them to usurp the role of parents? Admittedly, not all sex educators openly advocate that teenagers become promiscuous, but few teach the biblical injunction "Flee youthful lusts."

When the U.S. Supreme Court outlawed prayer and the Bible, the secular humanists in education seized the occasion to change traditional practices of teaching a value-laden education. They have told me, "Since religion has been expelled from our schools, so have God and morality." In other words, since morals are based on religion and since religion is no longer acceptable in our government-controlled schools, neither are moral values. Therefore, moral values may no longer be taught in many of our nation's schools.

Offering explicit sex education *without* moral values is worse than not teaching it at all, for it leads to experimentation with little or no restraint.

Explicit Sex Education

I led a campaign in California that helped to halt a radical course on sex education for kindergarten through grade twelve that was unbelievably explicit. Financed by the federal government to the tune of \$175,000, the program shocked everyone with standards of decency. Believe it or not, it called for the teaching of the details of intercourse to kindergartners. I have yet to meet a parent who wasn't incensed upon seeing the explicit nature of the material.

That single course, designed by "sexologists" employed at taxpayers' expense and taught to the state's sex-education instructors, proves one thing: We cannot trust the schools to formulate a sane and responsible form of sex education without close scrutiny by parents. In essence, we canot rely on our educators to protect the innocent minds of our children. Not all public educators are corrupt, of course, but the public has ample reason to distrust many of those in charge of such programs.

Sexual Values

No one has greater influence with teenagers than the mothers and fathers who have raised them. We must not permit the state or its self-appointed "saviors" to undermine parents and weaken their authority. Parents hold the keys to responsible behavior.

James C. Dobson, *Focus on the Family*, January 1987.

In my opinion, when some humanist sex educators refer to "teaching sex education," they really mean instructing young people in "the art of intercourse." Parents almost never mean that. In September 1979 a report entitled "The Impact of Life Science Instruction at George Mason High School, Falls Church, Virginia" was released by Columbia University. Financed by a grant from the Ford-Rockefeller Program in Population Policy, it exposed the *real* goals of most humanist sex educators. Summing up the indepth study, the report said, ". . . One goal of the sex education program is to alert students to the probabilities of pregnancy *and encourage only responsible sexual intercourse*, using contraception, if such sexual activity occurs at all" [author's italics].

Parents usually understand the term "sex education" to mean that their children need to know about hygiene, their own sexuality, and the fact that sex is to be reserved for marriage. The outcries of parental groups enraged by the advanced subject material taught to their children clearly indicate that some instructors use the public-school sex-education classroom to teach intercourse long before young people are old enough to bear the responsibilities for their actions. Surveys of today's high school students show that they are much more sexually active than when the current sex-education courses were introduced.

Until public educators recognize that teaching intercourse without benefit of moral values is overstepping their authority, parents should prepare themselves to offer proper information within the sanctity of the home. . . .

Sex education in the schools was promoted to parents as a means of solving social problems. However, the obsession with sex created by such classes has more than doubled the problems they promised to solve—which is typical of godless humanism's solutions to anything. It solves nothing but instead compounds the dilemma.

Children are born with two parents who are responsible to teach them about sex. The parents should never delegate that responsibility to a stranger, particularly one who teaches in an environment that is hostile to religion and moral values.

Few aspects of a person's life have greater impact on his future happiness than his sexuality. If he starts out improperly and becomes promiscuous, it will take divine forgiveness and several years to undo the consequences. In some cases, the results are irreversible.

Parents need to guard their children's sexuality and all teachings on that subject. No one has a greater stake in the future happiness, success, and development of a child than his parents. That is why parents should be the sex educators of their own children.

"The church, in particular, should reassert its role as the provider of sexual information and values to its children."

Sex Education Belongs in the Church

Kenneth Guentert

The Catholic church has long remained stalwart in its refusal to accept premarital sex, contraception, and abortion. Though the following viewpoint deals specifically with Catholic views, similar arguments for sex education in the church are used by many other religious institutions. The author of this viewpoint, Kenneth Guentert, writes for *U.S. Catholic* magazine. Guentert argues that parents often cannot communicate effectively with their children about sex so the church must provide accurate, moral instruction for its youth.

As you read, consider the following questions:

1. According to the author, why should parents not be held totally responsible for sex education?
2. How does Guentert think the church can serve as a check on the family?
3. In Guentert's opinion, how is the church ideally suited to provide sex education?

Kenneth Guentert, "Sex Education Belongs in Church," *U.S. Catholic*, August 1984. Reprinted with the author's permission.

Theologian Father James Burtchaell thinks that "standard sex education today tends to be morally bankrupt. It begins with a biological description of sexual function and fertility (known in the trade as the 'organ concert'), and it ends with indoctrination in contraception, abortion, and venereal disease. Basic to this pedagogy is the belief that youngsters will not accept moral ideals and should at least (or at most) be helped to cut their losses."

The above is not an argument against sex education; it is an argument for an alternative to the standard variety. I think the church should provide that alternative model.

Prudent Sex Education

And I have the Pope on my side. Or at least the Vatican Congregation for Catholic Education, which issued a document called "Education Guidance in Human Love" encouraging sex education. The document is important because it builds on a Vatican II decree that said, "As they grow older, (young people) should receive a positive and prudent education in matters relating to sex." As to who is responsible for sex education, the document said several times that sex education is the prerogative of parents but that clergy and educators are collaborators with them. But should parents be totally responsible for the sex education of their children? No. For one reason, the document doesn't say that; but let me give you my own reasons.

• *Even perfect parents need help.* By perfect I mean those fictional types who can communicate easily with their youngsters about you-know-what. Even perfect parents are up against the culture. They have to stack their values against the values their children receive from television, from music, from their peers, and from the schools.

One mother, whose 11-year-old is in my CCD [Confraternity of Christian Doctrine] class, told me that her daughter now has a boyfriend. "I'm not sure I like that," she said. I had to tell this woman that all the sixth-grade girls seem to be "going with" someone—although some of them are still children enough to not want the boy to know. That's peer pressure. The cool thing at this age is to be a "fox" or a "stud." To be sexy. That's peer pressure. By the time they get into high school they will be pressured, ready or not, to get rid of their virginity as something unwholesome. That's peer pressure—and it can be a lot more powerful than a parent working in a vacuum.

Sex on TV

Television bears much of the blame. Many parents complain about the sex and violence on prime-time television, but if a child watches one hour of daytime TV a week, he or she is likely to see plotlines based on adultery, rape, and even incest. Television alone, according to sex educator Sue Coppernoll, is an argument that parents cannot protect their children from outside sources of sexual information and values.

Music, if anything, is a more important influence on teen values. A few years ago I heard a sex educator itemize songs like Pat Benatar's "Hit Me With Your Best Shot" and ask, "Shouldn't someone teach these kids that sex can also be beautiful and gentle?" Perfect parents do, of course.

And many parents—along with Burtchaell—are suspicious or opposed to the "value-free" sex education of public schools that suggests, for example, that abortion and carrying a child to term are morally equal choices.

Parents can, of course, toss out the TV sets, confiscate the teenager's records, make rules against having boyfriends before the age of 12, review all public-school material ahead of time—or try to counteract this cultural blitzkrieg in the best way they can. It's not a job I would want to take on alone.

Communication Breakdown

• *Not all parents communicate easily about sex.* Some are uncomfortable. Some haven't been brought up to talk openly about sexual matters. Some simply do not communicate well. Some are ignorant. Some are gone. The rest are overwhelmed. A friend of mine is a single mother of 3 boys—11-year-old twins and a 14-year-old. She is a deeply Christian woman who receives no help from her former husband, an alcoholic. Her oldest boy is now strutting and jerking and rebelling his way through puberty, and she desperately wants to help him. The simple answer is, she can't. Certainly not alone.

A Healthy View of Sex

The evidence . . . suggests that at least one church sexuality program has the potential to provide comprehensive sexuality education for adolescents. The areas of values formation and clarity, alleviation of guilt, and the promotion of a healthy, balanced view of self as a sexual being are particularly salient issues.

The data indicate that a short term church-based sexuality program for high school adolescents can have positive effects on sexual learning and clarity of personal sexual values.

Lane H. Powell and Stephen Jorgensen, *Family Relations*, October 1985.

Teenagers present a special problem. Most parents I know can imagine answering even the sexual questions of little ones, but can't imagine doing the same to older children. One reason is that older children don't ask. They become more private, especially from parents, just as their bodies begin to change and their load of questions increases. Primitive societies allow for this phenomenon by insisting that young people choose a non-parent adult to help guide them toward adulthood. Modern teenagers likewise need non-parent adults to confide in (preferably adults who reflect the values of the parents).

The Community's Role

•*Children need the protection of the community; in particular, a high-quality positive sex education program.* Parents are the "primary educators" of their children, as documents say, but this should be understood as a duty that is often not fulfilled rather than as a right. Parents do not have absolute rights over their children. They cannot, for example, withhold from them an education and they cannot use them sexually. It is surprising how many parents—mostly men, but some women—sexually abuse children. According to Coppernoll, sexual abuse often occurs in families that isolate themselves from the larger community and try to gain all their emotional satisfactions from within. The community, which is a collection of families with common values, needs to act as a check on these families that isolate themselves. And one of the ways it does this is with a comprehensive sex-education program.

In turn, families have a role in establishing community standards and in checking the behavior of community members. Since children are often sexually abused by trusted members of the community, families have to act as a check on community members by training their children that they have a right to say no to adults who want to touch them, especially in certain places, especially in private. It can be done, especially with community help.

The church, in particular, should reassert its role as the provider of sexual information and values to its children but currently it is doing very little to help parents in this area. That's too bad because the church vision of sexuality is good. The church is, as Burtchaell says, "practically the only institution in the world that still thinks men and women can pledge themselves to one another for better or worse until death" and, I might add, have a romping, stomping good time while making the attempt. A Vatican document stresses that sexual intercourse has a two-fold value: an intimate communion of love between the couple and the fostering of children. Nowadays the "unitive" value, as theologians like to say, gets listed ahead of the "procreative" value. But both are still there.

A Pro-Life Stand

Moreover, a comprehensive sex-education program would be consistent with the Catholic pro-life position. If sexuality is the passing on of life—be it in the form of sexual intercourse or of other forms of creation—it follows that abortion is not an act of sexuality but of violence, that rape is not an act of sexuality but of violence, and that masturbation is as sexual as picking your nose. The idea of creating life is so essential to the way we think, as Catholics, that sex education should be a natural part of our religious-education curriculum. We don't need "sex courses"; we need to incorporate sex education into the curricula we have.

An Active Church

With sex education I think that the church should take an active part in helping young people to foster the growth of a good value system. It is difficult for youth today to differentiate between the better things—doing what is normally and ethically right, and doing the pleasurable thing that "everybody else is doing."

Paul Martin, *U.S. Catholic*, August 1984.

Second, the church has the infrastructure that can make a difference. We have schools, CCD programs, youth ministers and, most of all, parishes. The parish is accessible to families. They can have some say in the kind of sex education that goes on there. They can even help teach—with very little in the way of formal qualifications, which I consider a virtue.

Third, the church includes children in its vision of sexuality. It would be remiss if it did not show its care for them by answering their questions, by protecting them from abusive families and individuals, by offering them a community in which to play out their struggles toward maturity, and by passing on to them its own vision of the possibilities of human love.

Finally, if not the church, who?

*"We need to focus attention on reducing . . .
pregnancy among teenagers through a
comprehensive program of early sex education
in the schools."*

Sex Education Belongs in the Schools

Hyman Rodman, Susan H. Lewis, and Saralyn B. Griffith

Hyman Rodman is the director of Family Research Center at the University of North Carolina in Greensboro. Susan H. Lewis is an attorney. Saralyn B. Griffith is an instructor of child development and family relations at the University of North Carolina in Greensboro. Together, they analyzed numerous sociological studies on adolescent sexuality and concluded that teenagers have a right to reproductive information, contraception, and public health services through the schools. In the following viewpoint, the authors write that sex education in the schools does not promote promiscuity, while it does reduce pregnancy rates, corrects sexual misconceptions, and provides information about sex that parents cannot.

As you read, consider the following questions:

1. What proof do the authors give that teens are ignorant about sex?
2. According to the authors, why should sex education not be left up to parents?
3. In the authors' opinion, why do teens need sex education at an early age?

Hyman Rodman, Susan H. Lewis, and Saralyn B. Griffith, *The Sexual Rights of Adolescents.* Copyright © 1984 Columbia University Press. By permission.

We need to be forthright in advocating public programs of education in human sexuality. First, however, we must develop better educational programs, and better-trained teachers, so that we can be confident about the programs we advocate. One approach is to bring together experts from different disciplines and different value persuasions to develop the educational programs. If one discipline's facts are another discipline's myths, perhaps a third discipline can separate fact from myth. Then we shall see how much information we have about human sexuality that is not merely the ideological property of one discipline or profession.

In addition to the general advantage of reaching consensus about our knowledge of human sexuality—and assuming that we shall reach such consensus—there are a number of specific reasons for moving ahead with our recommendation. The first is to improve the knowledge of adolescents. At present there is considerable ignorance among teenagers, and that ignorance is costly. Close to half of all teenage women in the United States have engaged in sexual intercourse before the age of 18; approximately half of the women between 15 and 19 did not use contraceptives during their first experience with sexual intercourse; approximately one-fourth never used contraceptives; and fewer than half know when, during the menstrual cycle, they are at greatest risk of pregnancy. One could say, about such summary information, that there are small islands of knowledge in a vast sea of sexual ignorance. A properly planned program of education in human sexuality would be able to expand the islands and to shrink the sea.

Ignorance Is Not Bliss

There are substantial differences in knowledge according to age. Thirty percent of 15-year-old women knew when they were at greatest risk of pregnancy, in contrast to 34 percent of 16-year-olds and 47 percent of 17-year-olds. In a study by [G.L.] Fox (1979), 16 percent of 14- to 16-year-old daughters, and 41 percent of their mothers, correctly answered a question about when a women is at greatest risk of pregnancy. Unless we believe that ignorance is bliss, we should be able to agree that it is good to know the time of greatest pregnancy risk. And in an era when sexual interests and sexual messages are pervasive, we surely can find a way of teaching that knowledge. That specific objective in itself is, of course, limited. How well would the information be understood? How well would it be integrated with other knowledge about human sexuality? Obviously we oversimplify by singling out one item of information. But it is an example of an area where we can probably achieve consensus that knowledge is better than ignorance, and where we can reasonably expect to increase knowledge with the appropriate educational programs.

A second reason for our recommendation is that it would improve parent-child communication about human sexuality. There is widespread agreement among both parents and children that parents are a preferred source of sexual information. [S.M.] Bennett and [W.B.] Dickinson asked a sample of 18- and 19-year-old college students, "Who do you think should have the primary responsibility for teaching young people about sexual matters?" Parents were preferred by 76 percent of the females and 50 percent of the males; teachers were the second preferred group, listed by 13 percent of the females and 22 percent of the males.

© Margulies/Rothco.

Despite the pronounced preference for parents, however, parents are seldom identified by their children as an important source of information. For both sons and daughters, parents are almost uniformly listed as less important sources of information than teachers, and often as less important than either peers or the media. On such specific items as birth control and venereal disease, parents are especially low in importance as a source of information. Fox and [J.K.] Inazu report that mothers and daughters have greater difficulty in talking about birth control and sexual intercourse than about menstruation, dating, and sexual morality.

Since parents are a preferred source of sex information for children, it ought to be possible to develop a multifaceted educational program in human sexuality that will encourage better communication between parents and children. There is evidence that improved communication can be achieved if both parents and children are involved. Some parents are unable to accept the developing sexuality of their children, and parents and their children are often uncomfortable about discussing certain sexual topics. A program that incorporates human sexuality education and parent education should therefore be helpful. One advantage of increasing voluntary communication about human sexuality between parents and children is that such communication is associated with delayed sexual intercourse by teenagers, and with more consistent use of contraceptives once sexual intercourse is begun. . . .

Informed Decisions

A third reason for developing a multifaceted educational program in human sexuality, aimed at all age groups, is the known potential for competent decision making by early adolescents, and the need for information in specific areas in order to develop that potential. Since contemporary American teenagers must make many decisions about human sexuality, it is important to provide them with sound information upon which to decide. The educational program that we envision would provide such information and would therefore increase the competence and responsibility of adolescents' decision making.

One promising approach is a program that provides both information and practice at making decisions. [S.P.] Schinke, [B.J.] Blythe, and [L.D.] Gilchrist provided cognitive and behavioral training to a group of high-school sophomores: "Reproductive biology and contraceptive methods were covered by guest speakers' audio-visual aids, and Socratic discussions." Subsequently the students learned a problem-solving sequence, and were "guided through the sequence as they confronted decisions about dating, sexuality, birth control, pregnancy, abortion, childbearing, and parenthood." Compared to a control group, those who received training were more competent at dealing with human sexuality issues—showing more knowledge, better problem-solving abilities, and more effective patterns of interpersonal communication; in addition, six months after the training, they were "more favorably disposed toward family planning and were practicing more effective contraception than were control-condition adolescents."

Experience-based education can contribute significantly to adolescents' development. In a national study reviewing twenty-seven school programs, comprising such activities as voluntary community service and career internships, [D.] Conrad and [D.] Hedin conclude that experience-based education can have a positive impact upon the personal, social, and cognitive development of adolescents; among other things, these programs contribute to self-discipline and responsibility.

A fourth reason for the recommendation is the serious need for reliable information about human sexuality at an early age. Very young teenagers are engaging in sexual intercourse, often without using contraception, and are having unwanted pregnancies. These younger teens tend to have little knowledge about human sexuality, and poor communication with their parents. An effective program of education in human sexuality, through the schools or the media, could reach these teens, increase their knowledge, and perhaps improve their communication with parents. Radio and television advertising for contraceptives, if it could creatively combine educational with commercial goals, is potentially an important vehicle for reaching all age groups, including teenagers. One cannot expect media involvement in the near future, however, considering the results of a poll sponsored by the National Association of Broadcasters. They report that "most Americans would find television advertisements for contraceptives distasteful and embarrassing," thereby making the possibility of such advertising less likely.

Dealing With Reality

Those people who believe that sex education should be taught in the home—while voicing a fine idea—overlook the reality of the situation today. Research indicates that only about 10 percent of parents discuss sexuality with their teens beyond simply saying "don't." On the other hand, a 1982 study by Zelnik and Kim demonstrates that among unmarried sexually active teenage women, those who have had sex education courses have fewer pregnancies than those who haven't.

William H. Masters, Virginia E. Johnson, and Robert C. Kolodny, *Sex and Human Loving*, 1986.

Many young adolescents are little aware of the risk of pregnancy or of the range of contraceptive possibilities until after an initial pregnancy. More than 20 percent of all initial premarital pregnancies among teenagers occur during the first month of sexual activity; 50 percent occur during the first six months. Several researchers have drawn attention to the need to reach adolescents before they engage in sexual intercourse, or before their first pregnancy or their first child. An unwanted pregnancy or unwanted birth brings an adolescent to a professional agency where she has the opportunity to learn about effective contraception. But having the first child has a profound impact upon a teenager, and can permanently reduce her chances for education and employment.

One way to provide information to young teens, before they engage in sexual intercourse or become pregnant, is a strong and effective public program of education in human sexuality. In a study of 1,341 teenaged abortion patients in a Houston hospital serving an indigent population, [R.J.] Dworkin and [A.N.] Poindexter found that 91 percent used no contraceptives or used a contraceptive method improperly. Some, for example, used birth control pills sporadically, borrowing them from friends. The investigators concluded that we need to focus attention on reducing the probability of pregnancy among teenagers through a comprehensive program of early sex education in the schools.

Sex Education

In their 1979 national survey, [M.] Zelnik and [Y.J.] Kim report that approximately 75 percent of never-married women aged 15 to 19 had taken at least one course in sex education, and approximately 85 percent of these had learned about contraception in the course. One course is not a comprehensive program, and the percentages taking sex education, as reported by Zelnik and Kim, are higher than other estimates. For the adolescents surveyed, they report that taking a sex education course is not associated with sexual activity—that is, sexual intercourse took place to the same extent among those who had and those who had not taken a sex education course. Those who had taken a course, however, were more likely to have used some method of contraception at the time of first intercourse, and were less likely to have experienced a premarital pregnancy.

Research evidence suggests that comprehensive programs in human sexuality could lead to a reduced level of premarital sexual intercourse, especially among young adolescents, to more effective contraception for those who engage in sexual intercourse, and hence to a reduced rate of unwanted pregnancy.

A fifth reason for recommending educational programs in human sexuality is the evidence that such programs can be effective. In a thorough review of the impact of programs in sex education, [D.] Kirby, [J.] Alter, and [P.] Scales point out that, although the evidence is limited, it does indicate positive results. Most programs that have been evaluated have increased students' knowledge, "but they do not change the students' personal values that guide their own behavior." Some programs appear to have increased the use of more effective methods of contraception, decreased the use of ineffective methods, and decreased the amount of sexual intercourse without contraception.

"Unless sex education addresses values, ethics, morality, deferment of gratification, and goals, it is incomplete and potentially dangerous."

Sex Education Should Emphasize Abstinence

Donald Ian Macdonald

What message should sex education courses promote? Abstinence? Safe sex? Contraception? Parents, educators, and religious leaders continually debate this divisive topic. The author of the following viewpoint, Donald Ian Macdonald, believes teens should be encouraged to abstain from sex. Macdonald, the Administrator of the Alcohol, Drug Abuse, and Mental Health Administration of the Public Health Service, argues that sex education taught without moral and ethical values sends out conflicting signals. Macdonald writes that abstinence remains the appropriate message for most teenagers.

As you read, consider the following questions:

1. Why does Macdonald write that messages about "safe sex" are ambivalent and harmful?
2. According to the author, how does the abstinence message aid teens who are not sexually active?
3. Why does the author oppose sex education that teaches only "biology"?

Donald Ian Macdonald, "An Approach to the Problem of Teenage Pregnancy," *Public Health Reports*, July-August 1987.

More than 1 million American teenagers become pregnant each year. About half will deliver infants who are at greatly increased risk of mortality. A large percentage of the infants who survive will live with increased risk related to parental inadequacy. For the pregnant teenager herself, life will never again be the same.

The problem of teenage pregnancy has been addressed in a number of ways. Some of these have been ineffective; others have worsened the problem. In either case, our attempts frequently have reflected ignorance or misunderstanding of the forces which are associated with and contribute to teenage sexual activity. Consequently, we often have used the wrong message in education and prevention efforts and aimed it at the wrong target audience. . . .

Ambivalent Messages

The behavior of adolescents is very much influenced by the messages conveyed in the attitudes and practices of those around them, most especially their parents, peers, teachers, and the media that they hear and see. With regard to teenage sexual activity, abstinence is what we want from our children. Yet we often give ambivalent and confusing messages, as does a father who, while insisting that his daughter not engage in sex, urges her to use precautions if she must be active. Do we expect them to be abstinent, or don't we? When we seem willing to settle for less, we often get less.

The ambivalence reflects, in part, the belief of those advocating the message of sexual abstinence that it will not be heard or heeded by some teenagers. As inevitable as sexual activity is for some young people, failure to believe that abstinence is a realistic prevention objective for many others leads to mixed messages.

Uncertainty as to whether the message ought to be targeted to those adolescents who are likely to be abstinent or those who are not may result, in effect, in abandoning these youngsters who waver between choosing abstinence and sexual activity. In defining and promoting prevention models, we must take into account the great variations among children in age, gender, personality, potential for educational achievement, values, goals, environment, and other factors. No single message is likely to be effective for all.

In either case, the ambivalence which we convey may serve to encourage the very activity that we are trying to prevent. . . .

Weak Arguments

We can tell all children that they ought to remain abstinent, but if they must have sex, that they ought to be careful. This message is ambivalent and, thus, inherently weak.

A second option is to accept the fact that a large number of teenagers are or soon will be sexually active and concentrate on messages of "safe" sex. To accept the premises of this option, however, is to fall prey to two incorrect assumptions. One is the assumption that sexual activity has become the norm and that there is no turning back, or, stated differently, that the battle for abstinence has been lost, and there is no way of rolling back the rates. Second is the unproven assumption that sex education offered in accordance with a "safe sex" philosophy will be effective in reducing rates of teenage pregnancy.

With respect to the first of these, even in 1982, the year in which surveys recorded the highest rates of adolescent sexual activity, the assumption that most teenage girls were sexually active was true only for those 18 and 19 years old. More than 50 percent of the girls between the ages of 15 and 17 remained abstinent. Limited available data regarding sexual activity rates in boys indicate comparable patterns. Although more active than girls, only slightly more than one-half (56 percent) of adolescent boys were sexually active in 1977.

With respect to the second assumption—that we have lost the battle for sexual abstinence among adolescents—it should be noted that since the late 1970s, adolescent sexual activity rates appear to have leveled. Among black girls, rates leveled off in the period from 1976 to 1979 and have declined significantly since then. Among white girls, evidence of some leveling in sexual activity rates did not become apparent until the 1980s.

The third, and in my opinion, preferred, course of action is to adhere to the belief that the abstinence message is both reasonable

"TALK ABOUT <u>CONFUSING</u>... I STILL DON'T KNOW WHETHER THE <u>BIRD</u> OR THE <u>BEE</u> USES THE CONDOM!"

© 1987 Joel Pett, Lexington Herald-Leader.

and likely to benefit a significant number of young people.

"Just Say Later," the abstinence model, would build on gains seen in the recent leveling off of rates of sexual activity among adolescent girls. And of the three groups of teenagers described previously, it is likely that the one most readily amenable to efforts intended to encourage behavior change will be the swing group. This is not surprising.

In politics, advertising, and much of marketing, messages are most productive when aimed at the moderate or the undecided. The conservative Republican, for example, tends to count on the conservative vote and assume the liberal vote is not attainable. The vote that decides the election will come from the middle. To be successful, the candidate must tailor a campaign message that is credible and attractive to these swing voters.

Similarly, sex education will most easily change the behavior of those whose choice of whether to be sexually active or inactive is most open to suggestion—that is, the young girls who comprise the swing group.

The public health payoff of a "Just Say Later" prevention program which successfully encourages abstinence could be substantial. If the outcome were no more than a return to 1971 levels of sexual abstinence among teenagers, adolescent sexual activity rates would be reduced by slightly more than one-third (from 43 percent to 27 percent). In this context, it is noteworthy that pregnancy rates per 1,000 sexually active women have remained relatively constant from 1974 to 1982. Because the single most telling predictor of teenage pregnancy is sexual activity, we might anticipate a 33 percent reduction in teenage pregnancy rates. Significant reductions in infant mortality rates might follow.

Good Reasons for Abstinence

There is no shortage of good reasons for abstinence from sexual activity during adolescence. In fact, in crafting a message, a challenge often is to identify and emphasize the considerations most relevant in a given context. Some may emphasize the moral and ethical reasons, and the guilt which often is associated with teenage sexual activity. Others will point out that the educational and financial risks of pregnancy can be considerable. Another message may emphasize health risks—AIDS is currently the most visible, although by no means the only risk; another about which adolescents should be aware is the significantly increased morbidity and mortality of infants born to underage mothers.

Yet another message can note, from a psychological perspective, that sex with mutual consent, shared experience, and love does not routinely occur until around the age of 20. Prior to that age, sex is most often for self-centered gain; one's experiences and perception of sex can be harmfully shaped by such an early self-centered reward. Sex education curriculums in Sweden have begun to address the latter issue. Our messages have centered on warnings about personal risks and precautions to be taken, but the Swedish stress the importance of concern for others, including one's partner. An advantage of this message is that it permits, and even necessitates, that equal attention and emphasis be directed to the role and responsibilities of adolescent boys.

A Consistent Message

Why not say in schools to students exactly what most American parents say at home: Children should not engage in sexual intercourse. Won't our children better understand such a message, and internalize it, if we say it to them—and if we say it in school as well as at home? Why isn't this message being taught in more classrooms?

William Bennett, *Education Reporter*, February 1987.

For the majority of teenagers who are not sexually active, reinforcing the choice of abstinence may have immediate benefits. Teenagers want to belong and be accepted. When the prevailing assumption holds that most teens are sexually active, the abstainer may feel socially deviant. He or she may avoid activities in which a decision to remain abstinent labels one as "different." The abstinence model gives permission to say "no" and feel comfortable with that decision.

Sex Education

A societally sanctioned "rule of abstinence" also gives abstaining teens permission to encourage and shield others. Approaches that strengthen the peer community and give teen leaders support in their message of abstinence could bring tremendous results. . . .

However, no matter how successful we are, it is unrealistic to expect 100 percent abstinence. Earlier, in grouping adolescents by patterns of sexual activity, we identified a group of adolescent girls who have chosen to be sexually active. Should we give up on these 27 percent in order to focus on a group only half as large—the 16 percent who comprise the swing group? Of course not. For those committed to sexual activity, other messages and alternative approaches must be considered.

Some believe that the answer for the 27 percent of adolescent girls who are sexually active lies exclusively in an emphasis on education and contraception. We believe the complexity of the problem requires much more. . . .

The subject of sex education is controversial because it means different things to different people. If we are to resolve those differences, a useful first step is to look at the different components of sex education curriculums.

Many who are most concerned about teenage pregnancy and venereal transmission of disease feel that, when we fail to inform our children of possible protective measures, we are shirking our responsibility. Proponents of this view often reduce sex education to the provision of information about sperm, ova, the avoidance of fertilization, and the reduction of health risks associated with sex—for example, information about how the AIDS virus and other infectious agents may be transmitted sexually and instruction in preventing their transmission.

Teaching Ethics and Morals

I prefer to call information about pregnancy, disease, and their prevention, "biology" or "health-related instruction." As important as knowledge of anatomy and physiology may be, there is no conclusive evidence that education which presents such information has any effect in reducing rates of sexual activity and the array of related risks.

In my opinion, sex education involves much more than basic biology. Children's sexual practices are directly related to their perception of peer and societal norms, their attitudes and values, their hopes, their ability to defer gratification, and the protection offered them by their parents and others. Unless sex education addresses values, ethics, morality, deferment of gratification, and goals, it is incomplete and potentially dangerous. Without values we cannot teach responsible behavior.

"Educational programs which improve teens' use of contraception may ultimately save vast sums of money."

Sex Education Should Emphasize Birth Control

William A. Fisher

Many critics of sex education argue that providing birth control information to students gives them the green light to experiment sexually. William A. Fisher, a professor at the University of Western Ontario, disagrees with this theory. In the following viewpoint, he writes that most teenagers are sexually active before seeking contraceptive services. Fisher advocates integrating contraceptive information into sex education courses as a means of reducing teenage pregnancy and saving public health institutions millions of dollars.

As you read, consider the following questions:

1. In the author's opinion, why must sex education be taught in the schools?
2. What evidence does Fisher cite to prove that sex education does not promote promiscuity?
3. According to Fisher, how is contraceptive education a question of economics?

William A. Fisher, *Adolescents, Sex, and Contraception*. Hillsdale, NJ: Lawrence Erlbaum Associates, 1983. Reprinted with permission.

In the United States and Canada, contraceptive education has always been a politically and legally volatile issue. For example, when the physician Robert Knowlton published the first American book about birth control in 1832, he was sent to jail for 3 months at hard labor. Later, the Comstock laws made contraceptive education in the U.S. virtually illegal until 1936. At present, however, legal restrictions have eased, sex education has become more widely accepted, and a case can now be made for instituting contraceptive education in the public schools on a large scale.

Political advocacy of contraceptive education involves a two-part strategy. First, existing barriers—in this case, political opposition to sex education—must be removed. Then, favorable conditions—in this case, political support for sex education—must be instated. We will now discuss the removal of political barriers to contraceptive education, and some of the arguments that can be used to create political support for such education.

Dismissing Opposition

There are at least two political arguments against sex education that can now be dismissed on the basis of research evidence. First, many believe that the family—not the schools—is the appropriate setting for sex education of any kind. The research findings on this topic may be made clear to all parties concerned: most teens simply do *not* learn about sex at home. This does not seem to limit their sexual activity, although it may well interfere with teens' use of contraception. In essence, the home is now part of the problem of teenage sexual ignorance, and it may be unrealistic to believe that it can quickly become part of the solution. While parental input must be sought out and valued, school based programs may, for the present, be the most efficient means of providing sex education to teenagers.

There is a second argument against sex education that we can also judge in light of research evidence. Many are concerned that teens who know about contraception will become promiscuous, since they are equipped to avoid the consequences that are thought to deter other teens from having sex. Several kinds of data have been adduced to show that this is *not* the case. First, Elizabeth Allgeier [a researcher from Bowling Green State University] noted that most teens have sex first, and seek contraceptive information later. Thus, sex education could help prevent unwanted pregnancies among the many teens who are already sexually active but who remain uninformed about contraception. Moreover, studies of teens who have obtained contraception show increases in frequency of intercourse, but *not* in the number of partners with whom they have sex.

A second line of evidence concerning the presumed knowledge-promiscuity link comes from research that has directly

79

examined the effect of sex education on students' sexual behavior. For example, Zuckerman and his associates [clinical psychologists] found that college men who took a course in human sexuality increased somewhat their level of sexual activity. It is worth noting, however, that these men were *already* more permissive than a comparison group before the course began, they were quite a bit older (in their early 20s) than our intended public school clientele for sex education, and they had deliberately chosen to take the course in question. For these reasons, the Zuckerman, Tushup, & Finner findings may be quite limited in their generality. What, for example, might be the effects on sexual behavior of a *high school* course on family planning? Since this is precisely the intervention that we have in mind, the question is a critical one. Fortunately, a doctoral dissertation by Norman West focused on just this issue. Because it is one of the only studies to examine the effects of contraceptive education on the sexual behavior of high school students, we will discuss this investigation in some detail.

Contraceptive Information

Sex education courses vary in their attention to and treatment of contraception. In several European countries, however, sex education that provides information concerning contraceptive methods, including how to obtain them and how to use them, is associated with earlier and more diligent contraceptive use by adolescents, especially use of the pill.

The [Panel on Adolescent Pregnancy and Childbearing] urges that sex education programs include information on methods of contraception, how to use them, and how to obtain them.

Cheryl D. Hayes, *Risking the Future*, 1987.

In his doctoral research, West surveyed some 2,214 high school students in London, Canada. This sample included nearly 80% of all students then enrolled in the high schools that were chosen for study. About half of these students had taken a year long course in Physical and Health Education which, incidentally, included a "Family Planning Unit." As part of this unit, detailed instruction concerning birth control was provided, and in many cases actual devices (I.U.D.s, condoms, etc.) were passed around the classroom. In addition to the Family Planning Unit, it should be noted, quite a few of the students had also received some sex education in elementary school.

West classified each student in the survey with respect to whether they had taken the Family Planning Unit, or had received elementary school sex education. Self-reports were then obtained concerning the number of persons with whom students had sexual intercourse during the past 6 weeks. . . .

Data analysis showed that students who took the Family Planning Unit—compared to those who did not—had more sexual partners in the last 6 weeks. Does this mean that contraceptive education causes promiscuity among high school students? We think not, for two reasons. First, although the observed differences were statistically significant, practically speaking the differences seem to be trivial. All in all, students who took the Family Planning Unit reported something like .06 "more" sexual partners across a month and a half. Second, even the miniscule differences that did surface may well have been exaggerated by a tendency for permissive students to take the course, and for sexually conservative pupils to stay away. Whatever the ultimate cause of these differences, West's large-scale study provides an important piece of information. *At worst*, it seems that explicit contraceptive education may have only quite trivial effects upon high school students' sexual behavior. In light of such objective evidence, concern that sex education causes promiscuity seems to be unwarranted. . . .

Sexual Ignorance

Does present day education provide teens with the facts about contraception, so that they can make informed judgments about a matter that is of great importance to them? . . . Democratic principles notwithstanding—most teens do not have access to contraceptive education. This may occur as the result of action, as when a school board decides against sex education, or it may occur as the result of inaction, through failure to change the status quo. Either way, the result is sexual ignorance and the problems that derive from such ignorance.

It might also be mentioned that democratic principles would seem to require full and fair presentation of *all* relevant facts. The sex education which is available to teens, however, does not always conform to such standards. In fact, while curriculum guides for most subjects prescribe what *must* be taught, those for sex education classes may prescribe what must *not* be taught. Often enough, the verboten material involves information on birth control. For example, of those few teens who had sex education in high school, most were taught about sexual intercourse but most did *not* learn about contraception. This curious selection of topics is not unlike teaching student drivers about the accelerator, but avoiding all mention of brakes.

There is a second line of reasoning that advocates contraceptive education, and it focuses on the economic benefits to be derived from such action. It is a truism that present levels of contraceptive neglect are enormously costly. For example, in 1974 there were about 1,000,000 pregnancies to teenage women in the U.S. Some 210,000 of these pregnancies led to out-of-wedlock births, 280,000 were conceived before marriage but resulted in marital births, and about 270,000 pregnancies—mostly to unmarried teens—ended in abortion. These pre-marital conceptions, out-of-wedlock births, and abortions may be assumed to represent unwanted pregnancies. At $1,000 per birth and $250 per abortion, the total cost of dealing with these unwanted pregnancies in 1974 comes to $557,500,000 for medical procedures alone. This estimate is conservative, in that it does not include work days lost, the cost of complications, the expense of raising to maturity 490,000 children who were conceived before marriage, welfare costs, etc.

Needless Expense

It is interesting to compare this staggering expense to the cost-per-year for an equivalent number of women to be protected from pregnancy by oral contraceptives ($30,400,000), the diaphragm ($22,800,000), the I.U.D. ($38,000,000), or condoms and foam ($68,400,000; all cost projections are based on estimates). Theoretically, the effective practice of contraception could have saved at least $489,000,000 in 1974 alone. Needless to say, neither the limited resources of most teens nor the public coffers can easily bear this kind of excess expense. Thus, citizens and elected officials can be made aware of two facts. First, the status quo with respect to adolescent contraception involves extraordinary—and needless—expense. Second, educational programs which improve teens' use of contraception may ultimately save vast sums of money for individuals and for public institutions.

Deal with Reality

Some kids in the public schools are not going to be abstinent. It is unrealistic to expect them to change because abstinence is recommended. . . .

I haven't seen any evidence that teaching birth control increases sexual activity. Kids will engage, or choose not to engage, in sexual behavior whether or not they know about condoms.

Dorothy Williams, *Christianity Today*, April 17, 1987.

The cost saving potential of contraceptive education, incidentally, need not be used only as a general political argument that may one day lead to change. The same reasoning can be used to persuade specific health care institutions—who bear much of the excess cost just discussed—to take a more active role in contraceptive education. For example, if statistics were collected to show an insurance company or health maintenance organization that abortions were costing it X million dollars a year, they might be motivated to include contraceptive counseling as part of preventive health care for teens. What is more, the consumers of health care—to whom excess costs are also passed—may support contraceptive education as a cost saving measure.

Finally, it is worth noting that contraceptive education would expand the youth market for birth control products and result in profits for manufacturers, distributors, and retailers. Members of the private sector may thus be encouraged to support—politically and financially—programs in contraceptive education. In fact, it could be suggested that contraceptive neglect is largely a marketing problem that can be solved for the personal benefit of millions of teens and the corporate benefit of private industry.

An Educational Task

In summary, we have proposed arguments for removing political barriers to contraceptive education, and for creating instead support for these programs. It was pointed out that contraceptive education does not seem to have the deleterious effects that are often ascribed to it, and that teenagers in our democracy may be entitled to such education. Moreover, programs of this nature could save vast sums of money for health care providers and consumers, and contraceptive education may expand the birth control market and result in profit for the private sector. These arguments are examples of the sort of case that may be made to favor contraceptive education. They reflect our belief that eliminating sexual ignorance is a political as well as an educational task.

a critical thinking activity

Ranking Sex Education Concerns

The content and source of sex education information has become a long-standing controversy revolving around many arguments. The following activity will allow you to discover the values you consider important when teaching sex education courses. You and your classmates will decide whether or not to approach sex education from a moral standpoint or simply to present factual information. You will also decide which source of sex information you deem most appropriate.

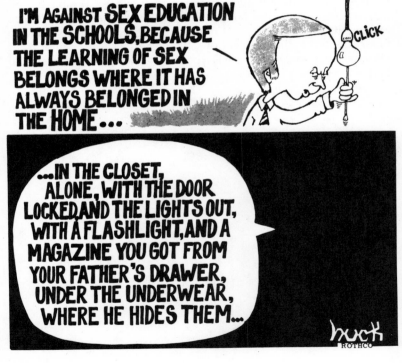

© Huck/Rothco.

Many religious leaders and concerned parents believe sex education should remain in the home where traditional values can be taught. Conversely, as the cartoon illustrates, others ridicule this notion that parents should be sex educators and argue that such teaching is best left to the schools.

Part I

Step 1. Working in groups of four to six students, analyze the following sex education concerns and rank them in order of the importance your group believes they should be given. Use number 1 for the most important concern, number 2 for the next most important concern, and so on.

Sex education should teach. . .

_____ the biology of reproduction.

_____ abstinence as a sexual alternative.

_____ the dangers of AIDS and sexually-transmitted diseases.

_____ marriage and family life.

_____ religious and moral values.

_____ the ability to say no to sexual pressure.

_____ that sex education is best taught in the home.

_____ about sexual deviance and sexual alternatives.

_____ the use of contraceptives and "safe sex."

_____ how to combat sexual abuse.

_____ the appropriate age at which sex is acceptable.

_____ how the teenage pregnancy rate can be lowered.

_____ sexual identity and sex roles.

Part II

Step 1. Remain in the same group and rank the sex education concerns as though you were parents of teenage children.

Step 2. Compare your group's answers with those of other groups in a classwide discussion.

Step 3. The entire class should discuss the following questions:

1. Did your answers vary between the two perspectives? Why or why not?

2. Would you rank the priorities any differently if you were a teacher? An unwed teenage mother? The leader of an over-populated nation?

3. How close does your school's sex education program come to your ideals?

Periodical Bibliography

The following articles have been selected to supplement the diverse views presented in this chapter.

William J. Bennett — "Sex and the Education of Our Children," *America*, February 14, 1987.

Mary Cartledge-Hayes — "A Mother's Day Challenge," *Ms.*, May 1987.

Jennet Conant — "How To Talk About Sex," *Newsweek*, February 16, 1987.

James J. DiGiacomo — "All You Need Is Love," *America*, February 14, 1987.

Madelon Lubin Finkel and Steven Finkel — "Sex Education in High School," *Society*, November/December 1985.

Sol Gordon — "The Case for a Moral Sex Education: A Response to Extremists," *The Humanist*, November/December 1987.

Fred M. Hechinger — "Teen-Agers and Sex," *The New York Times*, June 23, 1987.

William F. Jasper — "Teaching the Perversions," *The New American*, January 19, 1987.

Sharon Johnson — "School Sex Education Enters a New Phase," *The New York Times*, January 9, 1986.

Barbara Kantrowitz — "Kids and Contraceptives," *Newsweek*, February 16, 1987.

Asta M. Kenney — "Teen Pregnancy: An Issue for Schools," *Phi Delta Kappan*, June 1987.

Kim A. Lawton — "Responding to the AIDS Crisis," *Christianity Today*, April 3, 1987.

John Leo — "Sex and Schools," *Time*, November 24, 1986.

Allen J. Moore — "Teen-age Sexuality and Public Morality," *The Christian Century*, September 9/16, 1987.

Karen Sue Smith — "Sex Education: A Matter of Body and Soul," *Commonweal*, April 10, 1987.

Are School-Based Health Clinics Beneficial?

TEENAGE
SEXUALITY

Chapter Preface

School-based clinics are a collection of comprehensive health centers located at or near junior and senior high schools. Approved by local schoolboards, most clinics are sponsored by hospital or medical groups. Other sponsoring agencies include public health agencies, nonprofit organizations, school systems, and family planning agencies. Dr. James P. Comer, director of Yale University's School Development Program, describes school-based clinics as "the ideal place to expose [teenagers] to all they will need to function well as an adult. . . . Caretakers are in a position to form an attachment—to bond—to children. This bond will enable school personnel to motivate and teach children and will play a decisive role in a child's growth and development." It is this perspective—that clinic personnel act as nurturers and guides—that makes the school-based clinics issue so heated: they may be perceived as usurping parental authority.

The clinics either prescribe, dispense, or make referrals to other agencies for contraceptives. Supporters claim these services are necessary and cite the nation's high rate of teen pregnancies. They argue that because teens are sexually active anyway, they will be more apt to use the clinics' professional services if they are free and confidential. They see the clinics as a way of preventing the tragedy of children having children.

To critics, school-based clinics represent a dangerous assault on traditional family values. They charge that, because of Planned Parenthood's influence, the clinics promote abortion. They point to statistics showing that while the number of teens actually giving birth has declined as a result of the clinics, the number of pregnancies and abortions has increased. Many parents see this as proof that the supposedly morally neutral stance of the clinics is harmful. Instead of teaching students to think responsibly about sex, the clinics merely help them escape the unfortunate consequences of premarital sexual activity.

School-based clinics are a social experiment to prevent teen pregnancy. Are they a good idea? The authors in this chapter debate this question.

"Each of the measures . . . confirms the finding of a reduction in pregnancy rates among older teenagers and a halt in the rapid increases . . . in the rates among younger adolescents."

School-Based Clinics Are Effective

Laurie S. Zabin, et al.

Laurie S. Zabin, Marilyn B. Hirsch, Edward A. Smith, Rosalie Streett, and Janet B. Hardy are a group of physicians and researchers who conducted a study on the school-based pregnancy prevention program in the Baltimore school system. In the following viewpoint, the group concludes that positive changes in sexual knowledge and behavior patterns occur among teenagers because of the availability of contraception education and services. The group contends that school-based clinic programs are effective at reducing the teenage pregnancy rate.

As you read, consider the following questions:

1. What effect does the availability of contraceptives have on the beginning age of sexual activity, according to the researchers?
2. What behavioral changes do the researchers credit for reducing the pregnancy rate?
3. What factors about the Baltimore program itself do the researchers argue were crucial to its success?

Laurie S. Zabin, et al., "Evaluation of a Pregnancy Prevention Program for Urban Teenagers." Reprinted with permission from *Family Planning Perspectives*, Volume 18, Number 3, 1986.

In this article, we report on a school-based program for the primary prevention of pregnancy among inner-city adolescents that was designed and administered by the staff of The Johns Hopkins School of Medicine's Department of Pediatrics and Department of Gynecology and Obstetrics. The project was carried out with the cooperation of the administrators of four schools in the Baltimore school system—two junior high schools and two senior high schools. The program provided the students attending one of the junior high schools and one of the senior high schools with sexuality and contraceptive education, individual and group counseling, and medical and contraceptive services over a period of almost three school years. Students in the remaining two schools received no such services, but provided baseline and end-of-project data, and serve as the control sample. . . .

The Baltimore Study

Young men and women could enroll in the clinic and were eligible for the services as long as they remained in school. All services were free. Thus, both educational and medical services were available to the students. A single professional staff provided continuity and a bridge for young people between the school and the clinic setting.

The pregnancy prevention program began in November 1981. The clinic opened in January 1982, and services continued to be provided until June 1984. Throughout the duration of the project, the basic sex education curriculum, which is mandated by state law and is offered in all the junior and senior high schools in Baltimore, remained in place. . . .

The results reported in this article are based on the school populations as a whole, and do not compare the individuals who used the program services with those who did not. It is highly noteworthy, therefore, that the differentials are nonetheless statistically significant, and reflect a broad impact on the school community.

Accessibility Made the Difference

Over the course of the two and a half years that the program existed, changes in sexual and contraceptive knowledge occurred. These are both areas in which it has already been demonstrated that educational programs can make a difference. The rapid effect on clinic use exerted by an intervention program designed to supplement the basic sex education program already in place suggests that it was the accessibility of the staff and of the clinic, rather than any "new" information about contraception, that encouraged the students to obtain services.

Our study has shown attitudes to be somewhat more resistant to change than practice, but in this area there was less room for change to occur. . . . Support for adolescent childbearing or for casual sex was already very low in this school population before the program began. This seemed to suggest that more overall improvement was to be gained by helping students holding positive attitudes toward pregnancy prevention translate those attitudes into action than by attempting to change the attitudes of the few who do not share that view. With majority opinion already supportive of contraception and delayed childbearing, that is apparently what the program accomplished.

Did Not Encourage Sexual Activity

While the changes in the age at first intercourse are not large, they are substantial enough—in the direction of delay—to refute charges that access to such services as those provided by the program encourages early sexual activity. The program's ability to effect any further changes may well have been limited by the brevity of the project and by the age of the students when they were first reached. The fact that the age at first intercourse was delayed at all is impressive, and particularly important in view of the demonstrated high risks of early exposure to pregnancy.

Stop Children from Having Children

It would be wonderful if teaching teen-agers to say "no" could be a sufficient curriculum for adolescents, as the Reagan Administration suggests. But where the level of early adolescent child-bearing is one of the highest in the developed world, that is wishful thinking.

New York City can't afford such thinking, not when each year more than 14,000 teen-agers bear babies and adolescent girls have a 45 percent chance of getting pregnant. Programs like Baltimore's are now planned in 78 schools around the country. New York should try it too.

The New York Times, July 19, 1986.

Similarly, the results indicating that students attended clinics sooner after initiating sexual activity than had been the case are important. The project appears to demonstrate that if students in junior high schools are given access to nearby services and if they are offered information and continuity of care, they will use such services, and at levels comparable to those shown by older teenagers. That was clearly the case in this demonstration project, where confidential services were provided free of cost and in a sympathetic setting. Furthermore, the percentage of students going to a clinic or doctor before their first intercourse increased, as did attendance during the first months of sexual activity. Both these measures of preventive behavior were low at the time of

91

the baseline survey, as they were among clinic patients observed in an earlier study, and both increased markedly.

One of the most striking findings from the project is the demonstration that boys in the junior high school used the clinic as freely as girls of the same age. In view of the growing call for research into ways of attracting male clients to such facilities, the interest shown by these boys appears to be of some importance.

Increased Contraceptive Use

The changes in contraceptive use demonstrated by the evaluation are promising. Again, the results among the younger students suggest that early risk of pregnancy can be reduced with early attendance at a clinic. Use of the condom did not change consistently, but appeared to fluctuate with the use of female methods in such a way that the overall use of all methods requiring advance preparation increased significantly.

Increased and prompt clinic attendance and the resulting increased use of effective methods of contraception appear to have had a significant impact on pregnancy levels. The full extent of this impact may not have been fully realized by the time followup was completed. Each of the measures we used confirms the finding of a reduction in pregnancy rates among older teenagers and a halt in the rapid increases—by some measures, a decrease—in the rates among younger adolescents. In the face of rising rates in many U.S. cities, the marked reduction in pregnancy demonstrated here is to be welcomed.

As successful as this program appears to have been, a longer period than that involved here is probably needed to achieve and to measure the full impact of interventions such as these. Many effects may not be quick in coming, and although our study reports many significant effects, one would hope that with time, even more young people might be affected. Perhaps the evidence we present will encourage the investment of funds and energies in similar programs, over a longer term.

Combined School and Clinic Operation

Furthermore, early program exposure is clearly of some importance; interventions will have to take place before young people develop behavior that places them at risk of early, postpubertal conception. The effects of this program apparently were somewhat greater among younger than among older students. One of its major effects, indeed, is that it appears to have encouraged the younger sexually active teenagers to develop levels of knowledge and patterns of behavior usually associated only with older adolescents. This accelerated protective behavior, coupled with evidence that first coitus was not encouraged but, in fact, postponed, should provide solid support to the current movement toward the introduction of school-based clinics. The model described here is a combined school and clinic operation that offers full reproductive health services and that is located close to, but not in, the school. When two schools are close enough to share a clinic, this may be a particularly economical model; further analysis of the component services may suggest an even more parsimonious design that could achieve many of the same results.

Help Teens Avoid Getting Pregnant

Family planning is one of the best ways of reducing pregnancy, and we know that a vast proportion of adolescent conceptions, in particular, are unintentional. There's no doubt that the provision of clinical services can help cut down unintentional pregnancies among teenagers.

Laurie Zabin, *U.S. News & World Report*, September 29, 1986.

In conclusion, these findings suggest the efficacy of a program with pregnancy prevention as an explicit objective. Such a model requires a program and a staff capable of addressing a wide range of reproductive health issues. It does not preclude a broader range of adolescent health services (since these, too, are often badly needed), but it does suggest that meeting the sexual concerns, medical needs and contraceptive requirements of high school boys and girls is in itself an extremely challenging and demanding responsibility for program designers. More broad-based initiatives would, no doubt, have to include in their staffs some health educators, social workers, nurses or doctors with a strong commitment to the reproductive health of young people if they seek to replicate these results.

Constructive Preventive Behavior

Why did this program work? Access to high-quality, free services was probably crucial to its success. Professional counseling, education and open communication were, no doubt, also important. All these factors appear to have created an atmosphere that allowed teenagers to translate their attitudes into constructive preventive behavior. Precisely which separate components of the program contributed most to its success remains to be determined. Our understanding of similar school-based services for young people may well depend on the willingness of providers to scrutinize their interventions closely, on the ability of researchers to evaluate those interventions and on the cooperation of schools in making available the types of data needed to carry out such evaluations.

"The programs are more effective at convincing teens to avoid birth than to avoid pregnancy."

School-Based Clinics Are Ineffective

Stan E. Weed

Stan E. Weed is director of the Institute for Research and Evaluation in Salt Lake City. He conducted two major comprehensive studies with colleague Joseph A. Olsen to evaluate the effect school-based clinics have on teenage pregnancy rates. Their studies were published in the journal *Family Perspective*. In the following viewpoint, Weed states that his five years of research finds the number of pregnancies increasing along with the number of school-based clinics. He concludes that the programs reduce the live birth rate, but increase the rate of abortions. Thus, they appear to be more effective at convincing teens to avoid birth than to avoid pregnancy.

As you read, consider the following questions:

1. What does Weed state were some of the questions raised by the results of the first study?
2. What are some of the differences between the author's study and the Baltimore study that made them difficult to compare?
3. What efforts does Weed suggest society make to deal with the pregnancy problem in the future?

Stan E. Weed, "Curbing Births, Not Pregnancies," *The Wall Street Journal*, October 14, 1986. Reprinted with the author's permission.

More than a million teen-agers—most of them unmarried—become pregnant each year, and the number is rising. The belief is widespread that the number will be reduced by opening more "family-planning" clinics and making them more accessible to teens. However, research a colleague and I have done suggests otherwise.

Pregnancy Problem Has Grown Worse

As the number and proportion of teen-age family-planning clients increased, we observed a corresponding increase in the teen-age pregnancy and abortion rates: 50 to 120 more pregnancies per thousand clients, rather than the 200 to 300 fewer pregnancies as estimated by researchers at the Alan Guttmacher Institute (formerly the research arm of the Planned Parenthood Federation). We did find that greater teen-age participation in such clinics led to lower teen *birthrates.* However, the impact on the abortion and total pregnancy rates was exactly opposite the stated intentions of the program. The original problems appear to have grown worse.

Our research has been under way for two years, and analyzes data from such reliable sources as the Centers for Disease Control, the Guttmacher Institute and U.S. Census data for all 50 states and the District of Columbia. Since pregnancy, abortion and birthrates also vary with such factors as urbanization, mobility, race and poverty, these variables were also taken into account for each state. Our findings have twice sustained formal review by specialists in the field.

Our interest was prompted by the rising trends in teen-age pregnancy rates, despite large federal expenditures to help fund family-planning clinics and extend contraceptive services to teenagers. In 1971 the annual national expenditure (federal, state and local money) for these clinics was $11 million, and 300,000 of their clients were teen-agers. By 1981, the numbers were $442 million and 1.5 million clients. In 1972, the pregnancy rate for 15- to 19-year-olds was about 95 per 1,000. In 1981 the rate was 113 per thousand in that same age catagory. In that time period, when the size of the teen population was little changed, teen abortion went from 190,000 to 430,000. One must reconcile the rise in teen pregnancies with major program efforts that saw a fivefold increase in teen-age clients and a twentyfold, constant-dollar increase in funding.

Findings of Two Studies

Have the clinics just not reached enough teen-agers with these services to make a difference yet? Is the true and expected effect of family-planning services somehow being masked by other factors? Are clinics simply placed in the areas of greatest need, and therefore shouldn't we initially expect to see higher pregnancy rates associated with higher clinic availability? Would the teen-age pregnancy rate have been still worse without the clinics?

The importance of these questions and our original findings prompted a second study using additional time periods, data sets and analysis strategies. The findings and conclusions were very similar to those from the first study: lower teen-age birthrates, higher abortion rates, no reduction in teen-age pregnancy rates. All of the qualifying questions posed above were answered in the negative.

Apparently the programs are more effective at convincing teens to avoid birth than to avoid pregnancy. Birth avoidance can certainly be accomplished by resorting to abortion. Unfortunately,

Impact of Teen-age Family-Planning Programs

Projected vs. observed change in births, abortion and total pregnancies (per 1,000 teen clients, 1980)[1]

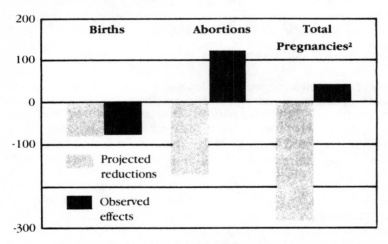

[1] These represent the remaining effects after accounting for race, poverty, urbanization and residential stability.

[2] Total pregnancy includes miscarriages, which are esti-mated at 20% of births and 10% of abortions.

Sources: Projected reductions (J.D. Forrest, Guttmacher Institute, 1984): Observed effects (Weed & Olsen, 1986)

that is not what the effort was set up to do nor the basis on which it was funded.

These findings would seem to be at odds with a recent widely carried report from two school-based clinics in Baltimore. But the studies are difficult to compare, in part because the published report from the school-based clinics is very brief, and therefore difficult to assess. In addition, ours is a national study looking at the net societal effects of a broadly implemented program of community-based clinics. The Baltimore study evaluates one program in two all-black inner-city schools. A single study of any one particular program has inherent limitations, both as a scientific statement and as a reliable guide for policy decisions.

Baltimore Study Is Questionable

Although the Baltimore study appears to be the first serious and rigorous attempt to evaluate a school-based clinic program, it leaves many questions unanswered. For example, over 30% (338) of the female sample dropped out between the first and last measurement periods. The size of the sample was small (96 girls had the full three-year exposure to the program). The reported survey data combine the clinic and non-clinic students, making it difficult to know exactly what the program effects were. The measurements of pregnancy, abortion, sexual activity and program involvement are not well specified and documented. All of this leaves us with questions about the results.

In a general way, however, both our data and the Baltimore study address the fundamental premise that greater accessibility and utilization of clinics is sufficient to reduce teen pregnancy. Our analysis of the national data suggests that any program based primarily on the notion of increased availability of contraceptive services must be examined and evaluated very closely, preferably by an independent party. This, as Planned Parenthood marks the 70th anniversary of its beginning, could trigger a significant shift in the nation's approach to the matter.

Strategies Must Change

What are the policy options available, given a recognition of the very real pregnancy problem at hand? First of all, we must be willing to admit past failures. Given the emotional and financial investment in the family-planning approach, that admission may be extremely difficult. But family planning for teen-agers is clearly not the first federal effort to be less successful than hoped nor the first to have effects other than those intended.

Second, the debate must turn to effectiveness. The various controversies and secondary issues attached to this subject can be addressed adequately only in this context. For example, clinic advocates maintain that parental notification and consent requirements will dissuade teens from utilizing the clinics and cause a major increase in teen-age pregnancies. Others argue that without this notice, parents are excluded from their rightful role and responsibility, and sexual activity is legitimized. But this argument becomes more relevant when we have clearly answered the effectiveness question.

When Facts Collide

Giving free contraceptives and abortions to teenagers *increases* the number of pregnancies. Yes, you read that sentence correctly. Publicly-funded contraceptives and abortions increase—do NOT reduce—the number of teenage pregnancies.

But how can that be? Isn't their very purpose to prevent pregnancies? And, isn't it logical to believe that more contraceptives will stop more conceptions? Maybe that's the motive of it and maybe that's the rationale of it, but the facts prove otherwise. . . .

When facts collide with purpose or rationale, reasonable people should face reality.

Phyllis Schlafly, *The Phyllis Schlafly Report*, February 1987.

Finally, future efforts must move beyond the narrow and unsubstantiated set of assumptions upon which previous efforts were based. The medical/technical solution of "responsible contraceptive behavior" appeared to be a simple and straightforward solution to a pressing public health problem. It was assumed that a trend toward greater sexual activity was inevitable and irreversible and that providing relevant information and contraceptives would be the optimal response. It hasn't been.

If future efforts are to be successful, they must take into account a broader set of influences and examine a wider variety of potential solutions to the teen-age pregnancy problem. Many factors in society are likely to have more influence on pregnancy rates than the lack or availability of contraceptive services. For example, other research has shown that enhanced educational and occupational aspirations (along with genuine opportunities for success) may well be more important than having access to birth control. These future efforts must also pay greater attention to the emotional and social development of teen-agers, how their value systems are acquired and changed, the emotional and economic incentives and disincentives to pregnancy, and teen-agers' sense of self-determination and control with respect to sexual behavior.

Awareness is growing that teen pregnancy is probably symptomatic of more fundamental factors in our society. There is also an increasing recognition that teen-agers may be more impulsive, have a shorter time perspective, and may be less likely to utilize adultlike decision-making processes. We can't expect teen-agers to use birth control devices and seek counseling in the same manner as mature adults acting rationally about sexual intimacy. Even married adults are not always consistent and rational when it comes to something as volatile as sexuality.

Finding a Lasting Solution

Any new directions in this effort will face the familiar, emotionally charged political and religious climate that surrounds the issues of teen-age sexuality, pregnancy and abortion. The teen pregnancy problem is real, however, and cannot be ignored. Lasting solutions will require more cooperation and a sense of common purpose, and less clinging to and defending of the current programs. Our youngsters and their children, born and unborn, will be the losers if we fail to break free of an ideological power struggle.

"School-based clinics should be opposed because their mere presence encourages promiscuity by their implied invitation to 'safe' sex."

School-Based Clinics Encourage Promiscuity

Mary Ann Kuharski

Mary Ann Kuharski is a Minneapolis free-lance writer whose articles have appeared in a variety of publications. In the following viewpoint, she argues that teens want relief from the pressures and complications of society's liberal attitudes toward sex. Kuharski believes school-based clinics should be opposed because they encourage teens to experiment with sex. She suggests that instead of providing contraceptives to teens, schools should promote a return to chastity which will give teens a greater sense of pride and self-worth.

As you read, consider the following questions:

1. How does Kuharski support her argument that teens are crying for relief from society's free-sex attitude?
2. What reasons does Kuharski give to explain why she believes chastity will work?
3. In what ways do school-based clinics weaken the public education system, according to the author?

Mary Ann Kuharski, "Teens Want, Need Chastity—Not Clinics," *St. Paul Pioneer Press & Dispatch*, January 21, 1987. Reprinted with the author's permission.

The values-free "safe-sex" promoters are at it again. This time, if they have their way, there will be walk-in clinics advising and prescribing for teens in every public high school in the nation.

While no one but the clinically insane would disagree with the need for pregnancy prevention among unmarried adolescents, there should also be no denying that all the efforts at "education," walk-in teen clinics, counseling (allowed without parental knowledge), contraceptives and abortion availability have only increased the number of young who now admit to experimenting with sex.

After two decades of a liberal "free-sex" diet, our teens are gasping and choking. Not for more—but for relief. The evidence of their rampant VD, including herpes, their increasing experience of contraception and abortion complications, including cervical cancer and infertility, and their tragic adolescent parenting is nothing less than a cry for help. We can stifle the cry by cramming them with more jams, jellies, pills and dangerous devices, or we can really care enough to instill some lasting values and standards that may enrich them for a lifetime.

I am suggesting nothing more radical than a return to chastity and promotion of that time-tested belief that sexual intercourse is to be cherished and reserved for marriage.

Chastity Will Work

Chastity will work where "protected" promiscuity, prescription pills and pregnancy scare tactics will not; and it will work because it is the only thing that offers young people something worthwhile to believe in and strive for—and there's nothing they like better.

Give these, the most idealist members of the human family, a race to run, a game to win, a goal to work toward—and no amount of self-sacrifice and discipline is too much.

It is they who will practice by the hour for musical or athletic contests. It is they who go to the Olympics while we sit home in easy chairs and watch with admiration. It is young people who staff the Peace Corps, VISTA, Guardian Angels and neighborhood youth groups. Their zeal and ability to give of themselves for others is unparalleled. Why, then, do we continue to deny them the opportunity to strive for chastity—a value that will benefit them long after medals of valor and championships have faded?

Teens Are Sold Short

We sell our teens short when we reward them for physical stamina, strength and endurance but offer only plugs, chemicals and "terminations" for their out-of-control sexual weakness. If we treat them as animals with no will-power or self-control, animals they will become. And where then is their sense of pride and self-worth?

Of course there are students for whom abstinence may be a remote concept. Even they, however, can rise to the challenge if their peers and instructors express a depth of faith and commitment in their ability—an expression sadly absent now. The hordes of young Americans drawn to cults is evidence of their eagerness to accept self-discipline and a high mode of conduct.

Ron Wheeler. Reprinted with permission.

Ignoring the demonstrated destruction of teen lives that has resulted from past experimental programs, including the utter failure (moral disaster, really) of contraceptive promotion, self-proclaimed "sex experts" now insist on the need for tax-financed "school-based clinics." That scheme would grant designated nurse practitioners and counselors the right to prescribe and advise for minors without their parents' knowledge. This is an invasive proposal sure to further weaken the public education system and drive more frustrated moms and dads to private institutions where parental responsibility is respected.

School-based clinics should be opposed because their mere presence encourages promiscuity by their implied invitation to "safe" sex.

"Sex oozes from every pore of the culture and there's not a kid in the world who can avoid it. To shut down school birth-control clinics in order to imply the contrary is a . . . costly excercise."

School-Based Clinics Do Not Encourage Promiscuity

Charles Krauthammer

Charles Krauthammer is a widely published syndicated columnist and a senior editor for the *New Republic* magazine. He received an M.D. from Harvard and practiced psychiatry prior to joining the *New Republic* in 1981. In the following viewpoint, Krauthammer contends that teens are promiscuous because they are immersed in a sex-obsessed culture. He argues that closing school-based clinics will not affect teens' morals or contain teenage pregnancy.

As you read, consider the following questions:

1. What does Krauthammer say are the two policy problems created by school-based clinics?
2. What examples does the author provide to show how the mass media encourages sex for teenagers?
3. Why does Krauthammer support school-based clinics?

Charles Krauthammer, "What Every Parent Must Know," *Los Angeles Times*, December 7, 1986. © 1986, Washington Post Writers Group, reprinted with permission.

The latest outrage of American life: The pill goes to school.
There are now 72 "comprehensive health clinics" in or near the
nation's public high schools. Very comprehensive. More than a
quarter dispense and more than half prescribe birth-control
devices. When the New York City Board of Education found out
that two of its clinics were in the dispensing business, it ordered
them to cease and desist.

Adults Can't Control Teen Sexuality

Secretary of Education William J. Bennett has waxed eloquent
on the subject. He is surely right that birth control in the schools
legitimates sexual activity and represents an "abdication of moral
authority." Clinics are not only an admission by adults that they
cannot control teen-age sexuality, but also tacit consent, despite
the "just say no" rhetoric.

Unfortunately, there are two problems: not just sex, but pregnancy. As in all social policy, there is a choice to be made. Is it
worth risking the implicit message that sex is OK in order to
decrease pregnancies? (Clinic opponents sometimes argue that
birth-control dispensaries do not decrease the number of pregnancies, a claim that defies both intuition and the evidence.)

Morals Are Not Learned at School

Bennett is right about the nature of the message. But he vastly
overestimates its practical effect. Kids do not learn their morals
at school. (Which is why the vogue for in-school drug education
will prove an expensive failure.) They learn at home. Or they used
to. Now they learn from the culture, most notably from the mass
media. Your four-eyed biology teacher and your pigeon-toed principal say *don't*. The Pointer Sisters say *do*. To whom are you going
to listen?

My authority for the image of the grotesque teacher and moronic
principal is "Porky's," the wildly popular teen sex flick that has
spawned imitators and sequels. My authority for the fact that teenage sex-control is an anachronism is Madonna. "Papa don't
preach," she sings. "I'm gonna keep my baby." The innocent in
the song is months—nine months, to be precise—beyond the question of sex. Her mind's already on motherhood.

Kids are immersed in a mass culture that relentlessly says *yes*.
A squeak from the schools saying *no*, or a tacit signal saying *maybe*,
is not going to make any difference. To pretend otherwise is to
misread grossly what shapes popular attitudes. What a school can
credibly tell kids depends a lot on whether they grew up on the
Pillsbury dough boy or on a grappling group of half-nudes fren-
zied with Obsession.

Time to face facts. Yes, birth-control clinics are a kind of surrender. But, as at Little Big Horn, surrender is the only sound
strategy.

Sex oozes from every pore of the culture and there's not a kid in the world who can avoid it. To shut down school birth-control clinics in order to imply the contrary is a high-minded but very costly exercise in message sending. Costly because the message from the general culture will prevail anyway, and sex without contraception means babies.

The Issue Is Pregnancy

The sex battle is lost. The front-line issue is pregnancy. Some situations are too far gone to be reversed. They can only be contained. Containment here means trying at least to prevent some of the personal agony and social pathology that invariably issue from teen-age pregnancy.

Clinics Can Help with Teen Pregnancy

Teens are sexually active, no matter how much distress that may cause their elders.

Shock and dismay won't help. Preaching won't help, either.

But there is still value in parents setting standards, and in being forthright and specific about how to say "no." There is also a point in helping teen-agers, boys and girls both, to take responsibility for their sexuality. . . .

There is a final point—the most difficult—in making birth control more accessible to young people.

An excellent model program already exists in four St. Paul high schools: the Maternal and Infant Care/Adolescent Health Services Project. . . .

The project's most important goals are to prevent that first teenage pregnancy; to avoid a second one if a first has occurred; to provide prenatal care as needed. Is it working? A single statistic is telling: The pregnancy rate has dropped 50 percent in those schools since the clinics opened, from 59 per thousand to 26 per thousand. . . .

Setting up such a clinic in every junior and senior high school is an idea worthy of the most serious consideration.

St. Paul Pioneer Press Dispatch, March 31, 1985.

Not that the sexual revolution can never be reversed. It can, in principle. In our time, the vehicle might be AIDS. The association of sex and sin elicits giggles. The association of sex and death elicits terror.

The coming counterrevolution, like all cultural revolutions, will not be made in the schools. It will happen outside—in movies and the news magazines, on the soaps and MTV—and then trickle down to the schools. As usual, they will be the last to find out.

I am no more pleased than the next parent to think that in 10 years' time my child's path to math class will be adorned with a tasteful display of condoms in the school's clinic window. But by then it will be old hat. The very word *condom* just broke through into the national consciousness, i.e., network TV. It was uttered for the first time ever on a prime-time entertainment show, "Cagney and Lacey." Condoms will now find their place beside bulimia, suicide, incest and spouse murder in every child's mental world.

If the schools ignore that world, it will not change a thing. Neglect will make things worse. In a sex-soaked culture, school is no shelter from the storm. Only a monastery is—if it doesn't have cable.

"In areas with high rates of teenage pregnancy . . . schools need all the outside help they can get; establishing clinics there may be one of the best ways to [assist] these children."

School-Based Clinics Can Control Teenage Pregnancy

Joy Dryfoos

Joy Dryfoos is an independent researcher, consultant, and member of the Board of Directors for the Center for Population Options. The following viewpoint is excerpted from her study of strategies for preventing teenage pregnancy. In it, Dryfoos describes the functions of school-based clinics. She maintains that parents favor the birth control clinics and concludes that providing contraceptive services in schools is effective in lowering the teen birth rate.

As you read, consider the following questions:

1. Dryfoos maintains it is important for family planning services to be based in the school or in nearby facilities. Why?
2. What are some other benefits that school-based clinics can achieve besides preventing teenage pregnancy, according to the author?
3. Dryfoos states that as the number of school-based clinics grows, they become less conspicuous. What does she predict their position will be in a few years?

In at least 14 American cities, comprehensive health services, including family planning, are being offered in clinics located in public schools or in nearby associated facilities. Other school-based clinics are in the planning stage. The first such program, the St. Paul Maternal and Infant Care Project, was established more than a decade ago. With little publicity, other school-based clinics have been organized independently in widely scattered locations, in response to local health needs. . . .

This article offers a description of . . . school-based health services and speculation on the potential of this type of program for preventing teenage pregnancy, decreasing student absenteeism and upgrading the quality of medical care. . . .

The School-Based Clinic

School-based clinics provide comprehensive health care, including family planning; they also generally employ social and educational approaches. Information from an informal survey of nine school-based clinic programs indicates that all offer physical examinations, such as for sports, employment, or general health screening, as well as treatment for minor acute illnesses, accidents and injuries. Each provides individual counseling about sexuality, gynecologic examinations and follow-up examinations for family planning patients. They either offer contraceptive prescriptions in the clinic or refer students to off-site birth control clinics. In addition, they perform laboratory tests, screen for sexually transmitted diseases (STDs), provide nutrition education and refer students with other problems to social service agencies.

More than half of the programs offer sex education to groups of students at the clinic itself, do pregnancy testing and provide prenatal care. Most also have programs for weight loss, treatment of drug and alcohol abuse, dental services, immunization and individual and family counseling. . . .

A few clinics dispense contraceptives on site and follow up users at home by telephone. Some clinics serve as a base for community outreach and education.

Clinics Used Equally by Males and Females

Caseloads vary from about 500 to 5,000 students, which represent anywhere from one-quarter to three-quarters of all students at the schools. Both male and female students take advantage of the programs equally. . . .

Most school-based clinics have emulated the St. Paul program, which was founded in 1973 by Laura Edwards, an obstetrician who became concerned about the consequences of high rates of teenage childbearing for the young mothers and their babies. Beginning with the existing Maternal and Infant Care Project, Edwards and the project staff sought and received permission from the local school board to offer prenatal and postpartum care, along with other reproductive health services, in a St. Paul inner-city junior-senior high school. . . . The program has demonstrated both a significant decline in births and high contraceptive continuation rates among participating students. . . .

Family Planning Services

High rates of childbearing among students often are cited as the rationale for initiating on-site health clinics, yet school-based clinics generally are presented as comprehensive, multiservice units that emphasize physical examinations and treatment of minor illnesses. This portrait certainly is valid, considering that only a small proportion of all clinic visits are for family planning. Nevertheless, in most clinics new patients (whether male or female) are asked at their initial visit if they are sexually active. If they are or plan to be soon, they are encouraged to practice contraception. If a young woman is interested in obtaining a birth control method, she is given a pelvic examination and a Pap smear as part of her physical examination. Contraceptives are generally prescribed following counseling. In a few schools, prescriptions are filled on the premises; in most, students are referred either to a collaborating clinic or hospital or to a local physician to have their prescription filled. Several programs provide only family planning information, counseling and referral. . . .

School-Based Clinics Are Successful

Clinics in St. Paul have *demonstrated that they are effective in reducing unintended births* and their effects. Their records indicate that over several years:

- the percentage of females receiving family planning services from the clinics increased from 0 percent to 33 percent;
- the 12-month and 24-month contraceptive continuation rates were 93 percent and 82 percent (based on 1982 data);
- the birth rates in the first school with a clinic dropped by about half and the birth rates in four schools which later opened clinics dropped by more than 40 percent;
- about 80 percent of adolescent mothers remained in school; and
- only 1.4 percent of adolescent mothers who remained in school had a repeat pregnancy within two years or until graduation.

Sharon R. Lovick and Wanda F. Wesson, *School-Based Clinics: Update*, August 1986.

Ideally, in programs that refer students to outside clinics for family planning examinations or prescriptions, the same nurse practitioner who attended the patient at the school clinic serves her at the other site, but it is often difficult to make this arrangement. In most cases, follow-up visits are encouraged. Almost all follow-up can be undertaken in school clinics, as family planning patients can be contacted easily in their classes and scheduled for follow-up visits. Confidentiality still can be maintained, because classmates do not know why the student is being asked to come to the clinic. . . .

Pregnancy and Abortion Counseling

Most of the school-based clinics provide pregnancy tests, and they generally offer pregnancy counseling and referrals to other agencies for maternity care or abortion. Many programs provide on-site prenatal care. Clinics funded through the Adolescent Family Life Act are prohibited from doing abortion counseling or making referrals. Those clinics generally offer pregnant students counseling about adoption, although most providers report that teenagers appear to have little interest in adoption. Other clinics either give students who want to obtain an abortion lists of facilities or make appointments for them. . . .

Male students appear very receptive to family planning education and counseling, according to program staff, and often request condoms where they are available. Male partners are also encouraged to participate in pregnancy counseling sessions when possible. . . .

School-based programs help to link health education and clinic services. Clinic staff often conduct sex education and family life classes in the school, so they have ample opportunity to encourage the students in the classroom to attend the clinic. . . .

Maintaining Confidentiality

Clinic personnel stress the importance of maintaining confidentiality. One difficulty is that while students' privacy must be respected, it is also important to gain the acceptance of parents, so that parents will permit their children to be treated in the school clinic. School-based clinics generally require parental consent before they will provide medical services to teenagers. In some clinics, parents are asked to sign a blanket consent form unrelated to any specific clinic visit. In others, the form lists each service, including family planning, and a student may receive only the services that have been checked. Most consent procedures apply for the entire period of the student's enrollment.

No clinic administrators report parental resistance to the signing of the form; neither have there been complaints thereafter. Their major problem has been getting the forms back from the parents. . . .

Judging from the lack of opposition, most parents appear glad to permit schools to provide health services for their children. Experience in family planning clinics shows that parents do not like to discuss contraception with their children and are relieved that their children are getting birth control from a reliable source. Program staff generally encourage parents to visit the clinic and, with the permission of the child, often speak with them about their children's problems. . . .

This preliminary overview reveals a number of positive aspects to school-based clinics. First, health services are provided where teenagers are. In the school-based programs studied, most health needs can be met within the clinic; if not, a student is referred elsewhere. Also, the students get consistent attention from a sympathetic staff.

Public Opinion Favors School-Based Clinics

In a 1986 poll commissioned by *Time* magazine, 84% of adults felt that school health clinics should make birth control information available to students.

A recent Harris poll of adults revealed that 67% are in favor of requiring schools to establish links with family planning clincs.

In Michigan, 80% of those polled in a statewide survey voiced strong support for confidential school-based clinics. Support was expressed by 82% of parents with children enrolled in public schools and 78% of citizens with no children in public schools. Nearly three-quarters (71%) of all respondents were in favor of the clinics providing birth control information; 40% were in support of clinics dispensing contraceptive devices to students.

In a Portland, Oregon telephone survey, 77% of school district residents who had heard about a school-based clinic opening in their community were in favor of the clinic.

In San Francisco, 93% of parents whose children were attending a school in which a clinic was proposed said they approved of the clinic concept and they would give their children permission to attend a clinic. Nearly half of the parents (45%) indicated a willingness to assist in the clinic's development.

School-Based Clinics, fact sheet from the Center for Population Options, January 1987.

School-based programs allow health education and promotion in the classroom to be combined with medical care and treatment in the clinic. Fragmented health and social services are brought together, and offered in a comprehensive way. These programs appear to be especially able to reach high-risk young men and women, who are least likely to use traditional health services. In addition, when family planning services are delivered within a context of comprehensive health care, young people can be sure that they will get contraceptives without being identified as sexually active by their schoolmates. A very important consideration is that contraceptive continuation can be enhanced by frequent contact and regular follow-up.

This type of clinic—organized and operated from outside the school system, yet on or near school grounds—can bypass laws that prevent school nurses from treating students for minor illnesses; this practice may improve students' general health, as well as their attendance. The school-based model also appears to be cost-effective, although estimated costs may be understated because of in-kind contributions from other agencies. Declining school enrollment has led to many empty classrooms, unused space that can be utilized by school-based clinics without cost to the school. . . .

Increasingly Popular

The number of school-based clinics probably will grow in the coming years, since they appear to be popular with students, parents, health and community workers, and school personnel. Indeed, after a few years, they lose their initially high visibility and become integrated into the school system, in a position similar to that of guidance offices.

As long as funding continues, school principals seem eager to provide health care to their students, especially in disadvantaged areas. The question, however, is stability of funding. . . .

Although it is not fashionable to suggest that long-term viability depends on federal funding, it is difficult to imagine that foundations will be willing to support these programs permanently, except for special studies. In the short term, it is clear that in communities with an interest in developing school-based clinics, an artful combination of private and public funding may at least adequately finance the initiation of services.

Clinics May Be the Best Way

This is not to suggest that a clinic should be housed in every U.S. high school. Many young people's health needs are well met by their family physicians, particularly in middle-class areas. More than 1.5 million young people already attend family planning clinics, and services offered in freestanding clinics probably are less costly than those offered through comprehensive programs.

However, in areas with high rates of teenage pregnancy, there are many adolescents who do not avail themselves of existing services. Preliminary analyses and anecdotal information suggest decreases in fertility and dropout rates and better attendance records in schools where comprehensive health and social services are available on site. It is not difficult to identify high schools with large numbers of adolescent mothers and substantial dropout rates. Such schools need all the outside help they can get; establishing clinics there may be one of the best ways to draw together the assistance that these children need to thrive, or even to survive.

"Studies have shown significant correlations linking . . . traditional values to lower rates of adolescent sexual behavior."

Traditional Values Can Control Teenage Pregnancy

Allan C. Carlson

Allan C. Carlson is vice president of The Rockford Institute, a conservative non-profit study center that focuses on the foundations of a free society. He is editor of the Institute's monthly newsletter *Persuasion at Work*. In the following viewpoint, Carlson states that the debate over the use of school-based clinics is really about morals rather than about the number of teen pregnancies. Carlson concludes that the solution to the adolescent pregnancy problem requires the social and moral reconstruction of American culture.

As you read, consider the following questions:

1. Why, according to the author, is it important for opponents of school-based clinics to see them as the logical culmination of the 20th century's birth control movement?
2. What is the sexual spiral that Carlson describes, and how does it relate to his contention that school-based clinics actually increase the number of teen pregnancies?

Allan C. Carlson, "The Sensual School," *Persuasion at Work*, July 1986. Reprinted with the author's permission.

Over a million American teenagers will become pregnant this year. Their situation generates ever more media and public hysteria and state scrutiny.

To an increasing degree, the solution of choice for the adolescent pregnancy problem is the school-based clinic. Local, state, and federal officials ponder the experiments found in 14 cities, where family-planning units disguised as "comprehensive health service" programs have been operating, with apparent positive results. . . .

The Problem Is Worsening

In its cover story on "Children Having Children," *Time* magazine highlights school-based clinics as the one institutional ray of hope for an otherwise worsening problem. At [St. Paul, Minnesota's] Mechanic Arts High, for example, the birthrate among female students fell from 59 per thousand in 1977 to 26 per thousand in 1984. The professional literature is even more adamant about the need for clinics nationwide. In his book *Unplanned Parenthood*, Frank Furstenberg Jr. concludes that the necessary "intervention strategies" of contraceptive education, pregnancy testing, and abortion counseling make schools the logical place for teenage "family planning" programs. Sociologist Susan Phipps-Yonas criticizes existing school sex education programs as too little and too late. Sex courses must begin earlier, she says, and be supplemented by contraceptive clinics on the premises. Another social scientist, Hyman Rodman, concludes that teenagers "typically engage in sexual activity whether or not they have access to contraceptives." Consequently, it "does not make sense to place obstacles in the way of their seeking contraceptives."

Birth Control and School Clinics

Such affirmations add to the policy drumbeats in favor of government funding of the clinics. In many parts of the country, though, parental groups are fighting tooth-and-nail against the innovation. They see the clinics as an insidious challenge to parental rights, an attempt by "professionals" to usurp control over their children's moral and sexual education.

In fact, school-based clinics and teenage sexual enlightenment represent the logical culmination of the 20th century's birth control movement, the last frontier of the contraceptive revolution. Opponents seeking to isolate and attack the clinics outside this broader perspective are merely flailing at a moving, impervious target. . . .

Seemingly conflicting findings cast light on the true situation in which we Americans find ourselves.

It might best be understood as a sexual spiral, where a growing national toleration of premarital sex and a breakdown of traditional restraints have resulted in ever more teenagers indulging in sexual activity. . . . In short, a spiral of more sexually active teenagers, more contraception, more sexual encounters per teenager, and some level of contraceptive failure would produce *both* a rising level of *averted* pregnancies and a rising level of *real* pregnancies, at least during the *transition phase.*

Seen another way, the United States is engaged in a great moral struggle, where traditional means of controlling teenage sexuality—parental regulation of dating and courtship, religious condemnation of sex outside of marriage, informal community controls such as the shame attached to an illegitimate birth—are being supplanted by a new social model. In this new scheme, children are cast as wholly independent moral actors, sexual activity is considered independent of marriage, and community use of stigma or shame is relabeled as illegal "discrimination." These two normative orders cannot coexist: each necessarily undermines the other. Clearly, the post-1960 birth control movement has aligned itself with the latter model.

Old vs. New Morality

The processes by which the "new morality" undermines the "old" are fairly obvious. School-based-clinic advocates, for example, are adamant on one point: adolescents have a "right to privacy" which overrides parental control. If the children want contraceptives, parents must not be informed without their off-

Dick Locher. Reprinted by permission: Tribune Media Services.

spring's consent. . . . At the family or neighborhood level, this same "right" has worked to destroy the traditional means of scrutiny by which parents or other elders governed the fertility of the young. With traditional controls so shattered, *only* the welfare state—in the guise of state-funded family planning clinics—remains to fulfill the role, albeit through radically different means.

On occasions, direct evidence reveals how the new morality of the birth control clinic destroys the old morality of family, church, and neighborhood. In a study of adolescent California girls, researchers compared young women's beliefs and behaviors before and after entering a youth clinic program and obtaining oral contraceptives. They found that 39.6 percent of the girls just entering the program disagreed with the statement "I enjoy participating in religious activities." Among those who had been involved for six-eight months, 56.2 percent disagreed. The change is in the direction one would anticipate: adapting one's behavior to the new moral order must result in greater dissatisfaction with the old.

The true conflict, then, is not over birth control. Rather, it is over the morality and the social norms governing family life, neighborhood, and community: the question of how we shall order our lives together.

Traditional Controls Still Work

What's to be done? To begin with, we can affirm that traditional controls over teenage sexuality still work effectively, when given a chance to function. Social research, as common sense, affirms that truth. For example, two researchers discovered that when measuring the relationship between family structure and premarital sexual behavior, black girls from father-headed families were *twice* as likely to be "non-permissive" sexually as compared to those from mother-headed units. Graham Spanier of Pennsylvania State University found that when mothers served as their daughters' primary source of sex information, the latter were significantly less likely to have engaged in coitus; when clergymen filled a similar role, the same was true for men. Other studies have shown significant correlations linking father-headed family structure, parental control over the sex education of their children, and traditional values to lower rates of adolescent sexual behavior.

We need also recognize the near universality of birth control practice and the futility of opposing (or even appearing to oppose) family planning. The need, rather, is to restore family planning to a normative model similar to that of the 1940's and 50's: birth control within marriage; abstinence as the normative expectation for unmarried adolescents; stigma or shame reattached to illegitimacy; and family planning as a private measure, conducted independent of federal encouragement or control.

It is clear that such social/moral reconstruction cannot be accomplished merely by political acts. While they are important, the broader infusion of sex into the whole of American culture must also be reversed. It has been estimated, for example, that the average television viewer witnesses in a given year over 9,000 scenes of sexual intercourse or innuendo on prime-time television. Rock lyrics commonly convey the same message. So do the "great novelists" of our time: Philip Roth, Norman Mailer, John Barth, and John Irving. A "counterculture" in these areas, and others, is needed.

Strengthen the Family Institution

Teenage pregnancy is not the problem. It is, rather, a symptom of the catastrophic collapse of the family in the bottom half of urban . . . America. . . .

Schools, which were once meant to assist families, now increasingly seek to displace families. Sex clinics are but the opening of another front in the public schools' war against families. . . .

Desperately needed are programs that strengthen rather than displace the institutions—beginning with the family—that have the primary mandate and potential for socializing the young. That, it seems to this writer, is the main message in the thoroughly justified protest against high-school sex clinics.

Richard John Neuhaus, *National Review*, December 5, 1986.

Large tasks? Yes. The sole practical alternative, however, is to complete the joint work of the frantic populationists of the 1960's and the feminist welfare-state-architects of the 1970's, and embrace the therapeutic sexual state. Contemporary birth control leaders such as Faye Wattleton are right: once they control enough schools and enough teenagers, and once parents with their troublesome old moralities are totally excluded from the picture, the movement *will* be able to bring the adolescent pregnancy rate down. The real debate, again, is not over that. It *is* over how we will choose to live together as a community and over the kind of people we shall be.

The choice made will have meaningful consequences. To choose but one, Joy Dryfoos notes chirpily in her commentary on clinics that "declining school enrollment has led to many empty classrooms, unused space that can be utilized by school-based clinics without cost to the school." These empty classrooms are, indeed, already the gift and the ironic legacy of the therapeutic sexual state.

117

"These clinics destroy the partnership between parents and school upon which responsible education is founded."

School-Based Clinics Must Not Undermine Parental Authority

William J. Bennett and Roger Mahony

William J. Bennett, secretary of education in the Reagan administration, is a leading spokesman against school clinics. In Part I of the following viewpoint, he warns that school-based clinics send the message to teens that parents can no longer effectively teach their children sexual responsibility. In Part II, Roger Mahony, archbishop of Los Angeles, contends that teaching human sexuality and religious values is a priority for most parents. School-based clinics destroy the traditional parent/school relationship by working against the wishes of most parents.

As you read, consider the following questions:

1. Bennett states that school-based clinics are a bureaucratic and offensive solution to the teen pregnancy problem. What arguments does he use to support his belief?
2. Why does Mahony support a strong religious influence in public school birth control matters?

William J. Bennett, in remarks delivered to the Education Writers Association in Baltimore, Maryland on April 11, 1986.
Roger Mahony, "School Based Health Clinics: A Pastoral Letter," published on October 28, 1986.

I

Another example: teenage, out of wedlock pregnancy. We have seen now in places around the country what I regard as a classic bureaucratic response to this problem: setting up birth control clinics in schools. Now this is obviously a local decision, but I would say this to any locality considering it: you had better be sure—really sure—that you have consulted fully and thoroughly with parents and the community. Or you may find that you have created a full enrollment policy for private schools.

The Wrong Kind of Response

And let me say more, if I may. Of course this is a local decision and not a decision for the Secretary of Education. It is a judgment not about birth control in general but about birth control in the schools. First of all, in my view, this is not what school is for. School should be predominantly and overwhelmingly about learning—about math and English and history and science. But even as an additional function of the school, it is my view that this response to teenage pregnancy—what I've described and talked about—is the wrong kind of response to the problem. It offers a bureaucratic solution—a highly questionable, if not offensive one—in place of the exercise of individual responsibility, not just by the children but by the adults around them. Further, it tends to legitimate the very behavior whose natural consequences it intends to discourage. And further yet, it encourages those children who do not have sexual intimacy on their minds to have it on their minds, to be mindful of it. Or it suggests to these young people that they're somehow behind the times. It thrusts upon those young people with scruples about sexual intimacy a new publicly legitimated possibility. And it does this in school. The child sees those in authority over him or over her acknowledging as commonplace what ought not to be commonplace and what parents do not wish, with good reason, to be commonplace. If individual parents wish, there are many other places to which they can take their children for professional help and guidance. But the wholesale use of the school is not the way to do it.

Clinics Mean Surrender

Birth control clinics in schools may prevent some births. That I wouldn't deny. The question is: what lessons do they teach, what attitudes do they encourage, what behaviors do they foster? I believe there are certain kinds of surrender that adults may not declare in the presence of the young. One such surrender is the abdication of moral authority. Schools are the last place this should happen. To do what is being done in some schools, I think, is to throw up one's hands and say: "We give up. We give up. We give up on teaching right and wrong to you, there is nothing we can

119

do. Here, take these things and limit the damage done by your actions." If we revoke responsibility, if we fail to treat young people as moral agents, as people responsible for moral actions, we fail to do the job of nurturing our youth.

II

There has been a concerted effort to establish health clinics in our nation's high schools. Now that clinics have been slated for four Los Angeles high schools—Los Angeles High, Jordan High, San Fernando High, and Culver City High—and several Los Angeles Unified School Board members are promoting these clinics in all district schools, I feel compelled to speak out on the matter.

While I share the desire of so many for free and/or affordable health services, I am in accord with those who question the wisdom of making public schools responsible for these services. In addition to many practical problems, since the rationale of these clinics is to offer a full range of birth control services and referrals for abortions, there are moral issues which we as Catholics must address.

The Better Option

What's wrong with sex education in the public schools? Just about everything, in the view of Secretary of Education William J. Bennett. Most such education, he recently told the National School Boards Association, lacks one crucial ingredient: It lacks any element of character. It rarely gets to questions of moral right and wrong. . . .

The schools have to stop being so neutral, Bennett told the school board members. "I think most Americans want to urge not what might be the 'comfortable' thing, but the right thing. Why are we so afraid to say what it is?" The overwhelming majority of parents would gratefully welcome the teaching of old-fashioned values of chastity, virtue, and sex in the context of marriage. "Let us from time to time praise modesty." . . .

Educators ought to rid themselves of the defeatist attitude that teenagers are going to "do it" anyhow, and the best way to curb pregnancy is to hand out contraceptives. Moral guidance is a better way yet.

James J. Kilpatrick, *Conservative Chronicle*, February 18, 1987.

First, the clinics will offer no lasting solution to the crisis of teen pregnancy outside of marriage. Technology alone cannot solve the human problems teens face at this critical stage of their development. While they are struggling with the forces of impulsiveness and peer pressure, they are still aware that sexual activity, and particularly pregnancy, is a matter of values. The presence of birth control clinics will serve to downplay the teenagers' need for responsibility by offering a false sense of independence.

Secondly, by making contraceptives readily available, the clinics' personnel will tacitly promote sexual relations outside of marriage for boys and girls, many of whom are barely in their teens. And when pregnancy does occur, as it does regularly in teens, including those who are using contraceptives, abortion becomes an alternative. As people committed to our Lord's commands, we cannot tolerate these options for our children.

Thirdly, these clinics destroy the partnership between parents and school upon which responsible education is founded. As the former Los Angeles School Board member Dr. David Armor has said, these clinics will "change the traditional relationship between the school and parent. It will work against the wishes of most parents, instead of with them, and our children will suffer the consequences."

Importance of Judaeo-Christian Ethic

Parental values will influence most teens, and educating young people to morally responsible views of sexual relationships, as designed by God for the covenant of marriage, is a priority for most parents. However, school birth control clinics send a message to students legitimizing behavior contradicting our Judaeo-Christian ethic. Their intrusion into public school education interferes with the rights of parents and their children to the free exercise of religious values. Teens will be able to make serious health decisions concerning the use of oral contraceptives, treatment of sexually transmitted diseases and abortion without parental involvement, and we will see the legitimate role of parents being undermined. It is no wonder William Bennett, the U.S. Secretary of Education said, "Such clinics open up the possibility of a wedge being driven between students and those who should have the greatest influence on them—their parents."

Finally, the very dignity of young people will be at stake. Clinics will reduce human sexuality, fertility and pregnancy to expressions of our humanity which can be controverted by pills or devices, and ultimately abortion. Such mechanical devices wound the sense of dignity given every person as a birth right, a sense so vulnerable in the impressionable years of adolescence. In addition, the misuse of sex or the choice to abort one's baby brings devastating spiritual, psychological and social effects, not to mention a lengthy list of possible dangerous physical complications.

What Parents and Teens Can Do

Rather than promote birth control and abortion, it is to be hoped that the high schools will present appropriate information on human development and sexuality and develop programs encouraging teenagers to value their sexuality and to say "No" to the abuse of sex, just as they have programs encouraging them to say "No" to the abuse of alcohol and the abuse of drugs.

I would like to remind parents and teens that many fine community resources already exist to help with family needs. Our own Catholic Social Services offers professional counseling and referrals for a wide range of needs, and you can confidently seek help there.

I would like to say directly to Catholic teenagers: God has a special love for you; your family loves you; and the Church loves you because of who you are. Treasure the person you are, and do not distort or weaken your personality by abusing alcohol, drugs or sex. To follow Christ and discover God's plan for your life will be a struggle, but it will release the "you" God created in the Divine image. In union with our Lord, Jesus Christ, you can be a powerful force for good in these troubled times, and I pray that you will treasure and take care of the life God has lovingly entrusted to you.

Finally, I urge our Catholic people and all those who value the family and have hope for the future of our children to join me in vigorous opposition to the placement of birth control clinics in our public schools. We have a right and duty to influence our communities in the interest of what we hold as human values. There are numerous channels through which we can exert powerful influence—through phone calls to public officials, letters, petitions, participation in public meetings, and in our private contacts with friends and associates. I am sure that in the months ahead many opportunities for involvement will present themselves, and I encourage each of you to meet this challenge.

8

VIEWPOINT

"The failure of parental authority is manifest in the almost 900,000 unintended teenage pregnancies in 1983."

School-Based Clinics Must Assume Parental Authority

Adam Paul Weisman and Donald E. Miller

Adam Paul Weisman is a reporter-researcher for *The New Republic* magazine. Donald E. Miller is the director of the school of religion at the University of Southern California, Los Angeles. They respond to the views of William Bennett and Roger Mahony in the previous viewpoint. In Part I, Weisman maintains that the great number of pregnancies proves that parental authority has failed to control teenage sexuality. Thus far, he contends, no effective alternative to school clinics has been established. In Part II, Miller concludes that the need to deal with the teen pregnancy crisis supercedes all arguments against birth control in the school clinics.

As you read, consider the following questions:

1. What are some examples that Weisman uses to show that school-based clinics are a good place to make contraceptives available?
2. On what basis does Weisman disagree with Bennett's position that birth control in clinics is an abdication of moral authority?

Adam Paul Weisman, "Clinical Examination," *The New Republic*, March 16, 1987. Reprinted by permission of THE NEW REPUBLIC, © 1987, The New Republic, Inc. Donald E. Miller, "When the Family Fails, Schools Must Step In," *Los Angeles Times*, November 11, 1986. Reprinted with the author's permission.

I

Should contraceptives be distributed to teenagers in public schools? A research panel of the National Academy of Sciences spent two years studying adolescent pregnancy in America, and decided they should. Its 1986 report, *Risking the Future*, prompted a new wave of angry debate about how to reduce the high rate of teenage pregnancy in the United States.

Two Distinct Camps

No one disputes the severity of the problem. Teen pregnancy ruins young lives and perpetuates a tragic cycle of poverty. According to the Alan Guttmacher Institute, the rate of pregnancy among American women aged 15 to 19 was almost ten percent in 1981. That far outstrips the next closest industrialized nation, England, where the rate is less than five percent. Guttmacher estimates that more than 80 percent of teenage pregnancies in the United States are unintended and unwanted. Every year about four in 100 women aged 15 to 19 have an abortion. But those looking for ways to reduce these statistics have divided into two distinct camps: one favoring contraception, the other, sexual abstinence.

The contraception advocates point out that a majority of teenagers have already rejected abstinence. In 1986, 57 percent of 17-year-olds say they have had sex. This camp believes that schools, as a central location in young peoples' lives, are a good place to make contraceptives available. Three recent studies (by the National Academy of Sciences, the Guttmacher Institute, and the Children's Defense Fund) have taken this view, while also calling for programs geared toward postponing adolescent sexual involvement and including parents in school sex education classes.

The abstinence advocates believe that answer lies in inculcating values based on a clear understanding that sex is simply wrong for teenagers. They say that moral lessons are best taught by parents in the home, but that schools should continue the job by teaching a chaste morality. Secretary of Education William Bennett has been the most outspoken proponent of this view. Exposing students to "mechanical" means of pregnancy prevention, he says, encourages "children who do not have sexual intimacy on their minds to . . . be mindful of it."

Baltimore and St. Paul Programs

Bennett concedes that "birth control clinics in schools may prevent some births." And indeed, whatever the drawbacks, the contraceptive advocates have one strong advantage in this debate: their approach works. The only rigorous study of a pregnancy prevention program for urban teenagers was conducted in Baltimore from 1982 to 1983 by researchers from Johns Hopkins Medical School. The Hopkins-run birth-control clinic, located across the street from one school and nearby another, reduced

124

the pregnancy rate in the schools it served by 30 percent while pregnancy rates in control schools soared 58 percent.

"Why did this program work?" asks Dr. Laurie Zabin, the program's director, in her report on the experiment. "Access to high-quality, free services was probably crucial to its success. Professional counseling, education, and open communications were, no doubt, also important. All these factors appear to have created an atmosphere that allowed teenagers to translate their attitude into constructive preventive behavior." . . .

These clinics also seem to help reduce unintended pregnancies. In St. Paul 33 percent of girls made use of the clinic's contraceptive services, and birth rates dropped by 50 percent. Thanks to the clinic's counseling, four out of five of the girls who did have children stayed in school, and only 1.4 percent of them had another pregnancy before graduation. Nationally, about 17 percent of teenage mothers become pregnant again within a year.

Schools Teach More Than 3R's

Bennett argues that distributing birth control is "not what school is for," and that doing so represents "an abdication of moral authority." Many educators have similar concerns. They fear that communities and government are trying to dump another social problem—like drug counseling and AIDS education—on the schools when they could better be handled in the home. Diane Ravitch, an adjunct professor of history and education at Teachers College in New York, says, "Schools are increasingly being pushed to be social service centers, and they don't do that well."

"What Family?"

When you consider the broken and disorganized families most of the kids come from, it's not surprising that the clinics' counselors and technicians often become *the best adult friends these youngsters ever had.* The vast majority of girls who become pregnant report alcohol and drug abuse, and often physical abuse, at home. They're desperate for affirmation, support, and guidance. When they get that kind of substitute family backing, they're quick to respond. . . . Against these front-line observations, it's almost laughable that Republicans in a U.S. House committee report on teen-age pregnancy said the problem will be solved by increased family responsibility that teaches children correct values and discipline. One has to ask: What family? [Emphasis added.]

Neal R. Peirce, quoted in *Crisis,* October 1986.

Yet clearly schools do more than teach students the three R's. Schools are where many teenagers learn to drive, weld, and cook. And numerous surveys reveal that over 80 percent of parents think it is a proper place for their children to learn about sex. Dr. Stephen Joseph, health commissioner for New York City, explains that if it weren't for the involvement of schools, the United States never could have achieved 100 percent immunization rates, a worthy goal that "wasn't perceived as the role of the school either at that time.". . .

Despite the success of Zabin's off-campus model, there is a good reason school-based clinics receive such wide support in the health services community: teenagers are notoriously lazy. As Cheryl Hayes, director of the NAS study explains, "If teenagers have to wait in the rain for a bus to take them to a clinic, there is a good chance they will never make it to the clinic." If the goal is providing health care and family planning services to teenagers, it is unlikely that anything will work as well as locating those services where most teenagers are: at school.

Of course the real question that excites people isn't whether teenagers should get birth control at school, but whether they should get it at all. There is no hard evidence linking exposure to contraception with promiscuity, and it is unlikely any teenager who watches prime-time television is less than "mindful" (as Bennett puts it) of sexual intimacy. Although Bennett has dismissed the recommendations of *Risking the Future* as "stupid," the opponents of making contraception available to teenagers have yet to offer an effective alternative. As for the "parental authority" that birth control availability is said to undermine, a 1986 Planned Parenthood survey of 1,000 teenagers revealed that 31 percent of parents discuss neither sex nor birth control with their children. The failure of parental authority is manifest in the almost 900,000 unintended teenage pregnancies in 1983. *Risking the Future* only makes that failure painfully clear.

II

Archbishop Roger M. Mahony recently issued a four-page pastoral letter challenging the appropriateness of instituting health clinics at four Los Angeles high schools.

He believes that these clinics, which would provide students with birth-control counseling and contraceptives, will legitimize premarital sex among teen-agers. He argues that health clinics will drive a wedge between parents and children by enabling students to make independent judgments about their sexual practices. He thinks that clinics will make teen-agers less responsible. And, of course, he fears that not only will artificial means of contraception be advocated but that abortion will be posed forcefully as an alternative.

The health-clinic issue raises many questions, including the appropriateness of the archbishop's pronouncement against them. Los Angeles school board member Jackie Goldberg responded to the charges by saying that "they (the Roman Catholic Church) have their own schools to run, and they don't have to take our advice and we don't have to take theirs.". . .

I believe that Mahony has the right to address issues that extend beyond the province of the Catholic Church. In fact, I believe that it is the obligation of the clergy to address the moral dimensions of all social policy decisions. If religion deals not only with the divine-human encounter but also with the quality of life for all persons—which I believe that it does—then the religious voice is appropriately present in national debates (as in the American bishops' pastoral letters on nuclear weapons and the economy) as well as in local debates about health clinics on our school campuses. The sacred and secular are not two isolated spheres; good theology sees them as always interpenetrating, one illumining the other.

Not All Teens Get the Message

Regardless of whether Michigan's plan for teen-age health care materializes, it is probably a generation late, said Maris A. Vinovskis, PhD, a professor of social history at the U. of Michigan. . . .

Dr. Vinovskis said that, per capita, the historic high point for teen-age pregnancy was not in the 1980s, 1970s, or even 1960s—but the mid-1950s. . . .

The important difference between then and now, Dr. Vinovskis said, is that in the 1950s most pregnant teen-age girls married. . . .

"Teen-age mothers who don't want to be forced into an early, unwanted marriage place a real economic burden on society," he said. . . .

Parents in other countries often are more open to discussing sex with their children than are Americans, and more willing for their children who are sexually active to use contraceptives, particularly birth control pills. . . .

Dr. Vinovskis suggested that teen-agers should be told firmly and unequivocally to avoid early sexual activity and be told of the possible consequences. But what of those who rebel against advice, or fail to hear it?

"Since all teens will not get the message, or will fail to comply, then access to birth control should be provided to them," he said.

American Medical News, March 13, 1987.

There is, however, more than one religious voice to be heard on the issue of health clinics in the schools. While I appreciate the arguments being made by the archbishop, the current crisis leads me to believe that health clinics are an appropriate com-

promise response to the 1 million teen-age pregnancies that occur yearly—75% of which are unintended, according to the
Children's Defense Fund.

Another Religious Voice

I view health clinics as a compromise response because if
parents were doing a better job of supervising their children and
teaching them the religious values that Mahony proclaims, we
would not have a situation in which half of all teen-agers are sexually active.

But the fact is that sexual activity among adolescents increased
by two-thirds between 1970 and 1980, and this increase is accounted for almost entirely by unmarried white women. Furthermore, the average teen-ager is sexually active for nine months
before seeking contraceptive advice. . . .

It is in the face of the failure of the American family that school
boards across the nation are proposing health clinics. While
Mahony expresses a legitimate concern about health clinics usurping a parental function, the opposing argument is that when
parents are not exercising their role, the schools are morally
obligated to expand their mandate.

Schools Must Step In

It would be wrong to think that the archbishop is the only one
worried about family life. The primary argument for health clinics
is to assist young people in getting a better start as parents. In 1982
half of all teen-age births were to single mothers. It is difficult
to imagine that many of these children are getting a very good
beginning in life, especially when we know that half of female-
headed households with mothers under 25 years of age have incomes below the poverty level.

Health clinics are not the entire answer, however. As the
Children's Defense Fund has noted: "The best contraceptive is
a real future." Full wombs among unwed teens are symptomatic
of empty hearts and failed aspirations. A health clinic can operate
for a mere $500,000 a year. The challenge of providing teen-agers
with a viable future and a reason to postpone the impulse of the
moment is a much more difficult task.

Distinguishing Between Fact and Opinion

This activity is designed to help develop the basic reading and thinking skill of distinguishing between fact and opinion. Consider the following statement as an example: "School-based clinics have been distributing contraceptives to teens since 1973." This statement is a fact which can be verified. But consider this statement: "School-based clinics are not the answer to the teen pregnancy problem." This statement expresses an opinion about the appropriateness of school-based clinics. Many parents and students may disagree with it.

When investigating controversial issues it is important that one be able to distinguish between statements of fact and statements of opinion. It is also important to recognize that not all statements of fact are true. They may appear to be true, but some are based on inaccurate or false information. For this activity, however, we are concerned with understanding the difference between those statements which appear to be factual and those which appear to be based primarily on opinion.

Most of the following statements are taken from the viewpoints in this chapter. Consider each statement carefully. *Mark O for any statement you believe is an opinion or interpretation of facts. Mark F for any statement you believe is a fact. Mark I for any statement you believe is impossible to judge.*

If you are doing this activity as a member of a class or group, compare your answers with those of other class or group members. Be able to defend your answers. You may discover that others come to different conclusions than you. Listening to the reasons others present for their answers may give you valuable insights in distinguishing between fact and opinion.

O = opinion
F = fact
I = impossible to judge

1. In 1986, 57 percent of seventeen year olds say they have had sex.

2. A birth control clinic run by Johns Hopkins University reduced the pregnancy rate in the schools it served by 30 percent.

3. School-based clinics are an insidious challenge to parental rights.

4. Birth control in the school encourages those children who do not have sexual intimacy on their minds to have it on their minds.

5. There are many alternative community resources available to teens that offer the same services and confidentiality as the school-based clinic.

6. There are now more than 70 comprehensive health clinics in or near the nation's public high schools.

7. Most of the school-based clinics offer pregnancy counseling and referrals for maternity care or abortion.

8. Parental notification and consent will dissuade teens from using the clinics and cause a major increase in teen pregnancies.

9. If teenagers have to wait in the rain for a bus to take them to a clinic, there is a good chance they will never make it.

10. Studies show that increased and prompt attendance by students at school-based clinics has had a significant impact on teen pregnancy rates.

11. Birth-control dispensaries in the schools do not decrease the number of pregnancies.

12. The Baltimore program was designed to address the health problems that are typical of many all-black, inner-city schools.

13. Sexually-active teenagers will use contraceptives if the school clinics provide them for free.

14. Most clinics stress complete confidentiality, assuring teens that their parents will not be notified.

15. The teenage pregnancy problem is real and cannot be ignored.

Periodical Bibliography

The following articles have been selected to supplement the diverse views presented in this chapter.

William J. Bennett ··· "The Case Against School-Based Clinics," *Crisis*, September 1987.

Bishop Bevilacqua "The Questions Raised by School-Based Health Clinics," *Origins*, September 3, 1987.

Mitch Finley "The Last Thing Teens Need Is Birth Control," *U.S. Catholic*, April 1987.

Randy Frame "School-Based Health Clinics: An Idea Whose Time Has Come?" *Christianity Today*, March 7, 1986.

William F. Jasper "After a Clinical Study," *The New American*, May 25, 1987.

William F. Jasper "Planned Parenthood: Its Solution to the Teenage Pregnancy Problem Is Contraception," *The New American*, November 10, 1986.

Sharon Johnson "Clinics Taking Birth-Control Help and Advice to the Teen-Agers," *The New York Times*, March 12, 1986.

The Nation "Papa Don't Preach," October 25, 1986.

Lynn Norment "Birth Control at School: Pass or Fail?" *Ebony*, October 1986.

Jean Seligmann "A Challenge to School Clinics," *Newsweek*, August 10, 1987.

Donna Steichen "Clinic Wars," *The New American*, August 1987.

Bill Turque "This Is a Good Place," *Newsweek*, February 16, 1987.

Lindsy Van Gelder and Pam Brandt "Beyond Sex Ed: School Clinics Tackle the Teen-Pregnancy Epidemic," *McCall's*, May 1987.

Adam Paul Weisman "Clinical Examination," *The New Republic*, March 16, 1987.

Pamela P. Wong "School-Based Clinics: Promoting Promiscuity," *Eternity*, March 1987.

How Can the Teenage Pregnancy Problem Be Solved?

Chapter Preface

Though American youth are no more sexually active than young people in other industrialized countries, the teenage birthrate of the US surpasses those of all other industrial nations. Currently, 400,000 American teenagers give birth each year.

Most health-care providers, educators, and politicians agree that teenage pregnancy is a serious problem. The economic costs alone are staggering. Unwed teenage mothers make up a disproportionate number of the nation's poor and subsist on government welfare programs such as Aid to Families with Dependent Children (AFDC) and food stamps. Unfortunately, most unwed teenage mothers come from families headed by single women who were teenage mothers themselves. Early motherhood often locks the mother and child into a cycle of poverty which is extremely difficult to escape.

Though many politicians and health-care officials have offered suggestions on how to decrease the teenage pregnancy rate, no cohesive national policy has been implemented. The authors in the following chapter present their solutions on how to solve this problem.

"If present trends continue . . . fully 40% of today's 14-year-old girls will be pregnant at least once before the age of 20."

Teenage Pregnancy Is Epidemic

Claudia Wallis

The United States has the highest teenage birthrate of any industrialized nation in the world. Many social commentators see no escape from the cycle of poverty for young mothers who cannot adequately support their children. In the following viewpoint, Claudia Wallis, an associate editor for *Time*, writes that Americans are finally realizing the social, political, and economic consequences of teen pregnancy. Wallis presents striking statistics concerning teenage pregnancy to suggest the seriousness of the problem.

As you read, consider the following questions:

1. According to the author, how do teenage mothers suffer economically?
2. Why does Wallis believe teen pregnancy is a difficult problem to solve?
3. In the author's opinion, why has single motherhood become more accepted?

Each year more than a million American teenagers will become pregnant, four out of five of them unmarried. Together they represent a distressing flaw in the social fabric of America. . . . Many become pregnant in their early or mid-teens, some 30,000 of them under age 15. If present trends continue, researchers estimate, fully 40% of today's 14-year-old girls will be pregnant at least once before the age of 20. Says Sally, 17, who is struggling to raise a two-year-old son in Los Angeles: "We are children ourselves having children."

Teenage pregnancy has been around as long as there have been teenagers, but its pervasiveness in this country, the dimentions of its social costs and the urgent need to attack the problem are just beginning to be widely appreciated. According to a Harris poll released in November [1985], 84% of American adults regard teenage pregnancy as a serous national problem. The news illustrates the growing concern:

• In Wisconsin, Governor Anthony Earl signed landmark legislation designed to combat unwanted teen pregnancies and, as he put it, to "limit thousands of personal tragedies that are played out in our state every day." The law, which won unanimous approval in the state legislature, provides funding for sex education in public schools, repeals restrictions on the sale of non-prescription contraceptives and provides $1 million for counseling pregnant adolescents. It also takes the unusual step of making grandparents of babies born to teenagers legally responsible for the babies' financial support. "All of us," said Earl, "young people and parents of young people, have a responsibility for our actions."

• At Chicago's DuSable High School, controversy erupted when school officials decided to establish an on-campus health clinic, authorized to dispense contraceptives to students who have parental permission. The school, which serves one of the nation's poorest neighborhoods, is battling a veritable epidemic: each year about one-third of its 1,000 female students are pregnant. The clinic has elicited picketing and protest, mostly by religious and antiabortion groups, but the school has refused to back down. Says Principal Judith Steinhagen: "All I can say is, we're trying to keep some young ladies in school and off welfare."

• The school board in Los Angeles announced that it too plans to open a health clinic offering contraceptives to high school students. So far, nine schools around the U.S. have taken this step, and others are expected to follow suit. Says School Board Member Jackie Goldberg: "There's an appalling number of teen pregnancies. I hope to upgrade the quality of teen medical care, and I hope that young men and women will consider the ramifications of being sexually active."

BABY BOMB

Such strong and controversial measures reflect the magnitude of the problem and its consequences. Teen pregnancy imposes lasting hardships on two generations: parent and child. Teen mothers are, for instance, many times as likely as other women with young children to live below the poverty level. According to one study, only half of those who give birth before age 18 complete high school (as compared with 96% of those who postpone childbearing). On average, they earn half as much money and are far more likely to be dependent on welfare: 71% of females under 30 who receive Aid to Families with Dependent Children had their first child as a teenager.

As infants, the offspring of teen mothers have high rates of illness and mortality. Later in life, they often experience educational and emotional problems. Many are victims of child abuse at the hands of parents too immature to understand why their baby is crying or how their doll-like plaything has suddenly developed a will of its own. Finally, these children of children are prone to dropping out and become teenage parents themselves. According to one study, 82% of girls who give birth at age 15 or younger were daughters of teenage mothers.

With disadvantage creating disadvantage, it is no wonder that teen pregnancy is widely viewed as the very hub of the U.S. poverty cycle. "A lot of the so-called feminization of poverty starts off with teenagers' having babies," says Lucile Dismukes of the Council on Maternal and Infant Health in Atlanta, a state advisory group. "So many can't rise above it to go back to school or get job skills."

Among the underclass in America's urban ghettos, the trends are especially disturbing. Nearly half of black females in the U.S. are pregnant by age 20. The pregnancy rate among those ages 15 to 19 is almost twice what it is among whites. Worse still, nearly 90% of the babies born to blacks in this age group are born out of wedlock; most are raised in fatherless homes with little economic opportunity. "When you look at the numbers, teenage pregnancies are of cosmic danger to the black community," declares Eleanor Holmes Norton, law professor at Georgetown University and a leading black scholar. "Teenage pregnancy ranks near the very top of issues facing black people."

The shocking prevalence of teenage pregnancy among white as well as black Americans was brought to light when the Alan Guttmacher Institute, a nonprofit research center in New York City, released the results of a 37-country study. Its findings: the U.S. leads nearly all other developed nations in its incidence of pregnancy among girls ages 15 through 19. As a point of comparison, AGI investigators looked at five other Western countries in detail: Sweden, Holland, France, Canada and Britain. Though American adolescents were no more sexually active than their counterparts in these countries, they were found to be many times as likely to become pregnant. And while black teenagers in the U.S. have a higher pregnancy rate than whites, whites alone had nearly double the rate of their British and French peers and six times the rate of the Dutch. Observes AGI President Jeannie Rosoff: "It's not a black problem. It's not just an East Coast problem. It's a problem for all of us."

It is also a complex problem, one that strikes many sensitive nerves. The subject of teenage pregnancy seems to raise almost every politically explosive social issue facing the American public: the battle over abortion rights; contraceptives and the ticklish question of whether adolescents should have easy access to them; the perennially touchy subject of sex education in public schools; controversies about welfare programs; and the precarious state of the black family in America. Indeed, even the basic issue of adolescent sexuality is a subject that makes many Americans squirm.

To understand the nature of the problem, one must look beyond statistics and examine the dramatic changes in attitudes and social mores that have swept through American culture over the past 30 years. The teenage birth rate was actually higher in 1957 than it is today, but that was an era of early marriage, when nearly a quarter of 18- and 19-year-old females were wedded. The over-whelming majority of teen births in the '50s thus occured in a connubial context, and mainly to girls 17 and over. Twenty and 30 years ago, if an *unwed* teenager should, heaven forbid, become pregnant, chances are her parents would see that she was swiftly married off in a shotgun wedding. Or, if marriage was imprac-tical, the girl would discreetly disappear during her confinement, the child would be given up for adoption, and the matter would never be discussed again in polite company. Abortion, of course, was not a real option for most until 1973, when the Supreme Court ruled it could not be outlawed.

A National Tragedy

More than a million American teen-agers get pregnant each year. About 400,000 of them will have abortions and a substantial number will miscarry. The 470,000 who do give birth will probably drop out of school, earn less than half than do those who become mothers in their 20's, and go on welfare. Their children are apt to have physical and development problems, and to give birth as teen-agers themselves. In 1985, those young families cost the Federal Govern-ment $16.6 billion in welfare, Medicaid and food stamps. And they pay the highest price—in lost opportunities.

Most Americans would agree that those facts add up to a national tragedy.

The New York Times, January 10, 1987.

All this has changed. Today if a girl does not choose to abort her pregnancy (and some 45% of teenagers do), chances are she will keep the baby and raise it without the traditional blessings of marriage. "The shotgun marriage is a relic of the past," observes Mark Testa, of Chicago's National Opinion Research Center. With teen marriages two to three times as likely to end in divorce, he explains, "parents figure, why compound their mistake?" In 1950 fewer than 15% of teen births were illegitimate. By 1983 more than half were, and in some regions of the country, the figure ex-ceeds 75%. Unwed motherhood has become so pervasive that "we don't use the term illegitimate anymore," notes Sister Bertille Prus, executive director of Holy Family Services, a Los Angeles adop-tion agency for pregnant teens.

With the stigma of illegitimacy largely removed, girls are less inclined to surrender their babies for adoption. In fact, fewer than

5% do (compared with roughly 35% in the early 1960s). "In earlier times if a girl kept her child, society would treat her like an outcast," reflects Sister Bertille. "The fear and guilt are not the same as before."

Unwed motherhood may even seem glamorous to impressionable teens. "They see Jerry Hall on TV, flinging back her hair, talking about having Mick Jagger's second [out-of-wedlock] child, and saying what a wonderful life she has," bristles Daphne Busby of Brooklyn, founder of the Sisterhood of Black Single Mothers. A succession of attractive stars, including Farrah Fawcett and Jessica Lange, have joined Hall in making a trend of extramarital pregnancy, something that 35 years ago helped get actress Ingrid Bergman blackballed in Hollywood.

But if unwed motherhood has lost much of its notoriety, premarital sex has over the same period become positively conventional. Like it or not, American adolescents are far more sexually active than they used to be. Guttmacher statistics show that the incidence of sexual intercourse among unmarried teenage women increased by two-thirds during the 1970s. Moreover, the sexual revolution seems to have moved from the college campus to the high school and now into the junior high and grade school. A 1982 survey conducted by Johns Hopkins Researchers John Kantner and Melvin Zelnick found that nearly one out of five 15-year-old girls admitted that she had already had intercourse, as did nearly a third of 16-year-olds and 43% of 17-year-olds. "In the eyes of their peers, it is important for kids to be sexually active. No one wants to be a virgin," observes Amy Williams, director of San Francisco's Teenage Pregnancy and Parenting Project (TAPP). The social pressure even on the youngest adolescents can be daunting. Says Stephanie, 14, of suburban Chicago, now the mother of a four-month-old, "Everyone is, like, 'Did you lose your virginity yet?'"

"The rate of teenage pregnancy has actually decreased during the past two decades."

Teenage Pregnancy Is Not Epidemic

Victor C. Strasburger

Victor C. Strasburger is a pediatrician from the Department of Pediatrics at the Yale University School of Medicine. In the following viewpoint, Strasburger writes that misleading statistics regarding teenage pregnancy have been sensationalized in the media. Strasburger believes that many studies concerning teenage sexuality are flawed. Teenage pregnancy, Strasburger contends, is no more prevalent today than twenty years ago.

As you read, consider the following questions:

1. Why does Strasburger question the results of surveys on teenage sexuality?
2. According to the author, what accounts for the decrease in teenage pregnancy?
3. How does Strasburger think the teenage sexuality statistics can be more helpfully interpreted?

Victor C. Strasburger, "Sex, Drugs, Rock 'N Roll: An Introduction." Reproduced by permission of *Pediatrics*, Vol. 76, page 659. Copyright 1985.

The denunciation of the young is a necessary part of the hygiene
of older people, and greatly assists the circulation of the blood.

Logan Pearsall Smith
Last Words, 1933

Whether one considers teenage pregnancy or teenage drug use,
the statistics appear alarming. Each year, for example, nearly 1.2
million female teenagers become pregnant: 49% deliver their
babies, 38% abort their pregnancies, and 18% have miscarriages
or stillbirths. Most of these pregnancies are unintended (74%) and
to unmarried teenagers (66%); 30,000 of them are to females 15
years of age or younger. Although female teenagers are biologically
capable of having healthy pregnancies (except for toxemia and
cephalopelvic disproportion in very young teenagers), they often
do not. Lack of adequate prenatal care results in a 6% death rate
of babies born to mothers younger than 15 years of age (2.4 times
higher than the rate for babies of women older than 20 years of
age). For women younger than 20 years of age, the maternal mortality rate is 8.5 deaths per 100,000 live births. (This last figure
compares most unfavorably with the risk of oral contraceptives
in this age group, which is estimated to be 1.1 deaths per 100,000
pill users, although, in fact, there have *never* been a single pill-
related death involving a teenager reported in the medical
literature.) Apart from the medical aspect of teenage pregnancy,
the social consequences can be equally devastating: An estimated
80% of pregnant teenagers drop-out of school; if they marry, they
face a 60% divorce rate within 5 years; and the repeat pregnancy
rate is 40% within 2 years.

Sexual Activity

Of course, the high teenage pregnancy rate is only a by-product
of the increased rates of sexual activity among American teenagers.
Since two Johns Hopkins researchers, Zelnik and Kantner, began
surveying thousands of teenagers nationwide in 1971, they have
documented a steady increase in the rate of premarital sexual intercourse: 30% of all teenage females surveyed in 1971, 43% in
1976, and 50% in 1979. The average age at first intercourse for
young women in the United States in now 16.4 years for whites
and 15.5 years for blacks. Predictably, the abortion rate and the
occurrence of gonorrhea have increased dramatically. Although
female teenagers make up only 16% of the childbearing population in the United States, they account for one third of all
abortions—400,000 annually. The Centers for Disease Control
received reports of 250,000 cases of gonorrhea in 15- to 19-year-
old teenagers in 1978, which was a quarter of all cases reported,
and an increase of 216% from 1960 to 1978. This represents an
incidence of 460 cases per 100,000 teenagers per year. Finally, for
those who claim that complete access to contraception is the

answer to the teenage pregnancy problem, one major study revealed that one of five teenagers becomes pregnant within the first month after her first sexual intercourse and 50% become pregnant within 6 months. . . .

The Good News

The statistics indicate that the "average" American teenager has a beer in one hand, a joint in the other, is lying in bed next to his girlfriend or her boyfriend, and will probably not complete adolescence without becoming pregnant, impregnating someone, or contracting gonorrhea. Without even considering other possibilities (automobile accidents, suicides, homicides), he or she appears statistically doomed. But is it so? Are all teenagers really the sex-crazed, beer-swilling, reefer-smoking refugees from outer space that many adults think they are? The data require a second look: the same studies that are used to indict teenagers for their excesses yield data that speak to their "virtuosity" as well.

Although both the Zelnik and Kantner and the Monitoring the Future [an annual survey of 17,000 high school seniors] surveys are elegantly constructed, are methodologically sound, and involve large population samples, they are still open to criticism. The Hopkins survey, for instance, involved only female teenagers in metropolitan areas, has not been repeated in the 1980s (due to lack of funding [J.F. Kantner, personal communication]), and has never been duplicated. The two other well-known surveys of teenage sexuality involved far smaller samples and were methodologically inferior. . . .

Good News

After peaking in 1980 the number of pregnancies to teens aged 15-19 has been declining, and in 1983 reached the lowest point since 1974. The pregnancy rate for women under 20 has declined from 114.0 in 1980 to 111.2 in 1983.

The birth rate for teenagers 15-19 has declined 8% between 1975 and 1984. This rate has dropped to the lowest level observed in the United States for this age group since 1940.

In 1984 teenage mothers accounted for only 13% of all births, the lowest percentage measured in the United States since 1957.

Center for Population Options, "Teenage Sexuality, Pregnancy, and Parenthood," January 1987.

Both the Zelnik and Kantner and the Monitoring the Future surveys are widely cited in the lay press as reflecting an "epidemic" of teenage pregnancy and teenage drug abuse. For the former, this is clearly not the case. For every age group except the younger than 15-year-old group, the rate of teenage pregnancy has actually decreased during the past two decades, although the rate of decrease has been slower than for the general childbearing population. With increasing rates of sexual activity, how can the pregnancy rate be decreasing? There may be changes in teenage fertility, particularly with increasing cases of pelvic inflammatory disease being reported, but certainly there has been increasing use of contraception and increasing availability and use of abortion. According to the Alan Guttmacher Institute, contraceptive use averts 680,000 teenage pregnancies per year; but consistent and more widespread use would prevent another 313,000. Other data from Zelnik and Kantner show a steady increase in the number of teenagers using birth control at first intercourse and at most recent intercourse: those always using contraceptives increased from 29% to 34%, whereas those never using contraceptives decreased from 36% to 27%. However, less reliable methods are being used. Use of the pill or intrauterine device decreased 40% at first intercourse, whereas the use of withdrawal doubled. At most recent intercourse, use of the pill or intrauterine device declined 50% whereas use of withdrawal increased 30% and use of the rhythm method increased 50%.

Interpreting the Statistics

More significantly, the same data that show increases in premarital sexual activity among teenagers can be turned around to appear, if not less frightening, at least hopeful: if nearly half of female teenagers have had sexual intercourse by age 17 years, half have not. Perhaps, instead of studying the "squeaky wheel," researchers should be looking at this unique population and trying to understand how these young women have successfully avoided the massive media and peer pressure frequently cited as being responsible for increased rates of teenage sexual activity. Furthermore, the same data do not really tell us how sexually active teenagers are. A 15-year-old adolescent who had intercourse once and now abstains is classified as being as "sexually active" as a 17-year-old adolescent who has intercourse three times a week with multiple partners. In fact, Zelnik and Kantner did look at this problem; their results are surprising: nearly 42% of the sexually active teenagers had not had intercourse within the 4 weeks before the interview, and another 25% of the teenagers had had intercourse only once or twice. In effect, the researchers unintentionally give support to the old double standard—once a teenager has had sexual intercourse, she is a statistically "ruined woman." Other data show that female teenagers are quite conservative in their numbers of sexual partners, with nearly one half having a single partner only and nearly 85% having no more than three partners.

Teenagers may also be more conflicted about their sexual activity than has been previously thought. A recent questionnaire given to 3,500 junior and senior high school students attending inner city schools in Baltimore during the 1981 to 1982 school year showed that 83% of sexually experienced teenagers cite a best age for intercourse older than the age at which they experienced it, 43% report a best age older than their current age, and 39% of females and 32% of males think that premarital sex is wrong. . . .

Encouraging Statistics

Every day more than 3,000 teen-age girls become pregnant, and 1,300 babies are born to adolescents. Five hundred teen-agers have abortions, 26 girls age 13 and 14 have their first child, and 13 others who are 16 have their second child. Over the course of a year, one of every 10 teen-age girls becomes pregnant.

Although the numbers from the National Center for Health Statistics seem bleak, in fact they represent a decline in the rates of both pregnancy and childbirth among women under 20. According to the center, the number of infants—479,000—born to teen-agers in 1984 dipped below half a million for the first time since 1960.

Nadine Brozan, *The New York Times*, March 14, 1987.

Clearly, there are ample data to support teenage sexual activity, pregnancy, and drug use as being major medical and psychologic hazards to today's American youth. However, no data are perfect. Studies—no matter how expertly done and how well publicized—need to be scrutinized carefully before conclusions are drawn about the deteriorating morals or hopelessness of today's youth or the impending decline of Western civilization. When this is done, the problems gain a sharper and deeper perspective: not all teenagers are sexually active, much less pregnant, and many teenagers disapprove of the same premarital sexual activity and the same drugs that adults do. Studies like these tend to be blown out of proportion by the national media (or by grant writers seeking to make their grant applications more appealing to review committees). As one pundit once said: "The 'teenager' seems to have replaced the Communist as the appropriate target for public controversy and foreboding."

"Improving [students'] academic skills . . . and their chances to graduate and get decent jobs serves to deter too-early parenthood."

Educational Programs Will Curb Teenage Pregnancies

Marian Wright Edelman

Marian Wright Edelman directs the Children's Defense Fund, an advocacy group dedicated to supporting the rights of minors. The following viewpoint is taken from Edelman's testimony before a Congressional subcommittee. In her address, she proposes the use of various educational programs to inhibit the rate of teenage pregnancy. Studies cited by Edelman indicate that students who drop out of high school are much more likely to become pregnant, or to impregnate someone, than those who graduate.

As you read, consider the following questions:

1. Why does the author advocate after-school learning programs?
2. According to Edelman, why is it necessary to keep students from dropping out?
3. Why does Edelman suggest that sex education be offered to younger students?

From *A Children's Defense Budget: An Analysis of the FY 1987 Federal Budget and Children,* copyright 1986, Children's Defense Fund, 122 C St. NW, Washington, DC 20001.

There is no single cause of or group affected by adolescent pregnancy. Changes in our families, our values, and our economy all have contributed to the tragedy of children having children. And just as there is no one reason for teen pregnancies, there is no "quick fix"—no single solution that offers a complete or adequate response to this complex problem.

The proposals that follow—an agenda designed to prevent pregnancies and to help more of our young people become self-sufficient adults—represent only a first and a partial answer to the challenge of adolescent pregnancy prevention. They constitute an agenda for government—federal, state, and local. . . .

After-School Programs

In a poll conducted by the Center for Early Adolescence, parents of ten- to fifteen-year-old children said that they were unsure of their young adolescent children's needs, fearful for the well-being of their children, and bewildered about what to do to improve the situation. Young adolescents are also at risk when left for long hours in unsupervised settings. Young teenagers may become pregnant, or get involved in drug and alcohol abuse or juvenile delinquency.

For low-income adolescents who may be struggling to stay in school but are falling further behind, after-school hours are an especially important time. These youngsters are not only vulnerable to negative influences, they are also more likely to be able to benefit from an enriched after-school experience. In short, with more and more women in the work force, it is becoming more and more important to structure good educational and recreational programs that offer to young adolescents constructive activities with peers as well as caring relationships with adults, both after school and during the summer.

Federal, state, and local funds must be provided for after-school programs for young adolescents. Legislative initiatives should provide authorization and funding to help communities start and operate a variety of programs that could be run by agencies ranging from schools to churches and community-based organizations. Community organizations also should explore the extent to which they can, within existing budgets, begin to develop after-school services in the interim.

By the time they reach high school, some youths have established a pattern of academic failure in traditional classroom settings. The cycle of poor academic performance, low expectations, and eventual resignation can take hold even in junior high and middle schools, particularly among children who do not receive strong parental support for academic achievement or whose families don't have the resources to give them the help they need outside of school.

Without diverse incentives for learning and opportunities to build self-esteem, through both in-school and out-of-school programs, these teenagers face high risks of dropping out and becoming parents at an early age. Improving their academic skills, their ability to keep up with their age group in school, and their chances to graduate and get decent jobs serves to deter too-early parenthood.

The absence of supervised and constructive activities for young adolescents in low-income communities during after-school hours also heightens the risk of teen pregnancies. Extracurricular programs can provide an important boost to the self-esteem of students who are struggling in school, while also ensuring adult supervision for children in their teens who have outgrown traditional child care arrangements but remain too young to be left alone.

An Educational Need

Given the number of teenage pregnancies and the consequences of these pregnancies for the mothers, their partners and their children, it is clear that, as a society, we need both policies and programs to deal with the enormity and complexity of this problem. . . .

We have not, as a society, developed national educational policies to deal with the prevention of pregnancy and the outcomes of adolescent parenthood. Neither have states taken an active role in proposing educational policies designed to assist communities confronting this problem.

Emily Stier Adler, Mildred Bates, and Joan M. Merdinger, *Family Relations*, April 1985.

Governments at all levels should address these needs by establishing community learning centers that combine remedial education activities with recreational, social, after-school, or vocational training programs serving at-risk youths. Grants under these new initiatives should be targeted to community-based organizations and youth-serving agencies that have demonstrated a capacity to reach poor and minority youths in out-of-school settings, including public housing sites. In many areas institutions of higher education should be involved.

The development of community learning centers would build upon the strong record of existing remedial education programs operated by some community-based organizations to serve out-of-school youths and adults who lack basic academic skills, promoting literacy and GED preparation. Separate part-time programs would encourage and reinforce academic gains for youths still in school. Providing these services during after-school and weekend hours, the centers would supplement the efforts of public schools and strengthen the awareness of at-risk youths that basic skills are essential to future self-sufficiency.

Dropout Prevention

Young people who fail to finish high school are at substantially greater risk of becoming parents at an early age. They also are considerably less likely than their peers to become self-sufficient adults. High school dropouts are almost twice as likely as graduates to be unemployed. Research suggests that school completion is one of the most important factors influencing youths' future employment, earnings, and capacity for self-support.

Particularly in low-income communities, however, much too large a share of our young people drop out of school, many at an early age. About one in four teenagers from poor families (regardless of race) fails to graduate from high school, compared to one in twelve non-poor students. In major urban areas with large concentrations of poor youths, high school dropout rates frequently exceed 40 percent. This alarming dropout problem reflects the many difficulties confronting public schools in low-income neighborhoods: inadequate resources, limited opportunities for parental and community involvement, and low morale and expectations among teachers and administrators. . . .

Sex Education

Today's children are growing up in a world far more complicated and demanding than it was even thirty years ago. Teens normally are expected to delay the traditional markers of adulthood—completion of education, entrance into the labor force, marriage, and family formation—in order to accommodate needs for increased education, career exploration, and training. At the same time, however, we are placing greater demands on teenagers. Decisions made at ages thirteen, fifteen, and seventeen often play a crucial role in determining our youths' adult success—decisions about high school completion, college or vocational training, careers, and, most important, parenthood.

Too few teens are being offered sufficient adult guidance in making these important decisions. Even fewer are being given instruction in how to make good decisions, or sound information about the importance of doing so. Too many teens drift into decisions that they later regret.

The decision to become sexually active, because of its potential long-term consequence—parenthood—is perhaps one of the most important decisions an adolescent will make. Two-thirds of a sample of adults recently polled believe that parents have little or no control over this decision, and that, while family education and communication are key elements in sex education and pregnancy prevention, the schools have an important role to play. The link between sex education and teen pregnancy prevention has been well documented. For example, an international study conducted by the Alan Guttmacher Institute clearly suggests that sex education (and the provision of contraceptive services to sexually active teens) has little effect on rates of sexual activity among teens but does encourage sexual responsibility and, consequently, reduces teenage pregnancy rates.

Stay in School

More of our youths are recognizing the pitfalls of too-early sexual activity, too-early parenthood, and failure to graduate from school. The proportion of teens who are becoming parents is decreasing slowly. Still, too many teens, male and female, are taking steps that may limit their chances of adult self-sufficiency. . . .

To change teens' behavior, we must give them a sense of hope and options for the future. A teen's ultimate chance of success as an adult is determined by two factors: awareness of opportunities for success in the adult world that are meaningful and likely to be available, and adequate preparation to meet the adult world's challenges.

Karen J. Pittman, *Preventing Adolescent Pregnancy and Building Youth Self-Sufficiency,* 1987.

The availability, quality, and timeliness of life-planning programs currently vary tremendously across and within states. Reflecting the central role that state governments traditionally play in setting standards for educational practice, this initiative would establish state initiatives in support of life planning and decision-making curricula in public schools, including a state mandate that all public school students receive such instruction (including age-appropriate sex education) at elementary, junior, and senior high school levels.

While many school districts offer some instruction on physiology, pregnancy, and childbirth, few offer students an opportunity to get this information early—before they become sexually active—and in a context that strengthens their decision-making skills. Only two states—Maryland and New Jersey—and the District of Columbia now require that school districts offer life planning/sex education programs.

Family Education

Many elements of this initiative would require state leadership and policy guidance but little or no additional state expenditures. Broad goals and minimum requirements for life planning/sex education programs would be incorporated in state law and regulation.

The development of specific curricula, however, would be left to local communities and school districts, many of which have the beginnings of adequate family life education programs already in place. Community involvement in the development and review of curricula would be encouraged, and the rights of individual parents would be protected through provisions for excusing students at parental request. Technical assistance in identifying and adapting model curricula that have proven successful in strengthening decision-making skills and encouraging teens to delay pregnancy would be offered by the state to local school districts.

The acceptance and the effectiveness of these programs depend heavily upon adequate training for teachers so they have both the information and the comfort with this sensitive topic necessary to teach it well. Therefore, this initiative also would provide state financial support to in-service teacher training programs, including workshops, courses, and seminars led by community professionals. This training effort should be coupled with the establishment of state certification procedures to ensure that teachers have sufficient knowledge to present life planning/sex education curricula. Finally, this initiative would encourage the development of related programs sponsored by community-based professionals and organizations that would reinforce efforts in schools and provide the curricula in out-of-school settings.

"We suggest that . . . teenage girls actually receive periodic payments for remaining childless."

Paying Teenagers To Remain Childless Will Curb Teenage Pregnancies

Jay Belsky and Patricia Draper

Social scientists have proposed answers to the teenage pregnancy problem ranging from sex education courses to school health clinics to providing free contraceptives. In the following viewpoint, Jay Belsky and Patricia Draper offer the unique solution of paying teenage girls not to have children. Though the program may initially be expensive, they argue, the American taxpayers will eventually save money on welfare payments while offering teens a brighter future. Belsky, a professor of human development, and Draper, an associate professor in the Department of Human Development and Family Studies, both teach at Pennsylvania State University.

As you read, consider the following questions:

1. According to the authors, what can the US learn from China's reproductive policies?
2. How would Belsky's and Draper's plan work?
3. Why do Belsky and Draper think this program will be economical?

Jay Belsky and Patricia Draper, "Reproductive Strategies and Radical Solutions." Published by permission of Transaction, Inc. from SOCIETY, Vol. 24, No. 3, March/April, 1987, pp. 20, 23, 24. Copyright © 1987 by Transaction, Inc.

Few would argue with the contention that being born with AIDS is among the worst calamities that could befall a newborn infant in the world today. Nor would anyone wish upon an infant a childhood characterized by severe scarcity of food and heightened susceptibility to disease, as is all too routinely experienced by hundreds of thousands of infants in so-called undeveloped countries around the world. As a nation we pride ourselves in the belief that it is the availability of opportunity in the face of abundant natural resources (one of which is people) that insures our own prosperity and keeps such ecological disasters far from our shores. Yet in view of what we know about the incidence and consequences of unwed, teenage motherhood in this society, particularly when it occurs in a context of economic deprivation, it is hard to believe that the United States does not already face a demographic calamity.

Not only are teenagers who have children—especially those under fifteen or sixteen—likely to drop out of school, have more children before they are twenty, and become dependent on welfare assistance; but their offspring are at heightened risk for poor health, school failure and, as adults, unemployment and underemployment. . . .

A Need for Solutions

To disregard the need for special treatment of children of unwed, impoverished teenage mothers (as well as their married counterparts) is to fail to recognize both the lost opportunities of fully developing humans and the exorbitant cost of poorly developed ones. The latter cannot read, cannot hold stable jobs, are susceptible to drug and alcohol abuse, are at high risk for becoming criminals, for having more children before they turn twenty, for becoming welfare-dependent, and for generating more offspring at high risk for these same adverse—and societally costly—developmental outcomes. . . .

Should we conclude, given the extent to which a variety of intertwined biological and social processes maintain high rates of teenage parenthood in economically impoverished sectors of our society, that little can be done to modify the current state of affairs? Although our answer to this question is no, we qualify this by noting that change will come neither easily nor inexpensively. The experience of modern China convincingly demonstrates that birth rates can be affected by social policies; however, several important features of the Chinese situation must be noted. The first is that men, not just women, are committed to one-child families. Even if American teenage girls were inclined to control their fertility while in high school, it is often in the reproductive interests of teenage—and adult—males for teenage girls to have their children. China also offers strikingly tangible benefits to households that limit family size and imposes equally explicit costs upon those that do not. In the context of a totalitarian society such social control is effective.

The United States is not a totalitarian state and does not aspire to become one. We value liberty such that any effective policy must work within the constraints of these cultural values. But if we followed part of China's lead, and employed the carrot even if not the stick, might it prove feasible to reduce the incidence of teenage pregnancy and parenthood among unwed, uneducated, and impoverished adolescents in the United States? The answer to this question must currently be "we simply do not know," since most policy initiatives . . . focus upon adolescents who have already become parents, and those programs that seek to prevent pregnancies really offer few incentives other than those inherently associated with remaining childless. Since teenage parenthood brings with it reproductive and social-psychological benefits—not just to the teenager but to her kindred as well—for prevention to succeed, one set of benefits must take the place of those already existing. We propose such an alternative benefit plan, one which we recognize to be both radical and expensive. Because we cannot be certain of its effectiveness, we advance this plan principally to provide some illustration of the kind of effort that might be required to stimulate planned social change.

Periodic Payments

We suggest that adolescent development zones be established in which teenage girls actually receive periodic payments for remaining childless. These zones would be defined on the basis of demographic data identifying areas in which teenage parenthood can be considered to have reached epidemic proportions.

Jay Belsky and Patricia Draper, *Society*, March/April 1987.

When it comes to urban development, proposals are often advanced regarding the establishment of urban enterprise zones in which businesses pay lower taxes and receive additional financial benefits for establishing themselves in areas known to have extremely high rates of unemployment. Parallel to this idea, we suggest that adolescent development zones be established in which teenage girls actually receive periodic payments for remaining childless. These zones would be defined on the basis of demographic data identifying areas in which teenage parenthood can be considered to have reached epidemic proportions. The payments themselves would be designed to reward teenagers for managing their reproductive behavior during their adolescent years in a manner that should not only benefit the well-being of

153

their children when they have them, but also reduce the costs that society ultimately pays for supporting all too many teenage mothers and their offspring.

How might such a system work? We can imagine young adolescents, receiving when they turn eleven (and six months later) a cash payment of, say, $50 if they report to the school nurse and can be certified, simply on the basis of external (visual) examinations, as not being pregnant. When these girls turn thirteen this twice-a-year award would increase to $75. At fifteen payments would become both larger and more frequent, with teenagers receiving $100 every four months. Teenagers remaining childless until eighteen years of age would qualify for a cash bonus of $500. Graduation from high school would carry with it an additional $500 cash bonus along with $2,000 in educational benefits to be used to secure additional training (academic or vocational) within the next two years.

Parental Aid

As is true of other social changes our nation has experienced, we must recognize that generational tension and conflict is likely if teenagers begin on the basis of this program to behave in ways that are clearly different from the ways in which their parents and other relatives structured their life courses. Since kindred often have a strong stake in teenagers becoming pregnant, we presume that for the prevention effort to be maximally effective, it must bring immediate and tangible—not just delayed and long-term—benefits to the families of teenagers as well. Efforts that are not sensitive to this need for kin benefits run the risk of failing in their stated goal of reducing the incidence of teen parenthood, or, even worse, of creating immediate, enduring, and ever-damaging conflict and tension between teenagers and their kin. From the standpoint of reproductive biology, to say nothing of social psychology, relations among nuclear and extended family members are a primary resource to be preserved and protected by policy initiatives, even if initially threatened [by] policies such as those we have outlined.

Benefits to Parents

What all this suggests is that the families of teenage girls should be rewarded when their daughters manage their reproductive behavior by delaying pregnancy and childbirth. We propose that the mother or legal guardian of a teenage girl residing in our adolescent development zones receive cash payments of $250 if the teenager is childless at age twelve, $400 if still childless at age fifteen, and $600 if she reaches the age of eighteen without having become pregnant and borne a child. To insure that the future possibility of such benefits does not encourage women to have children, mothers would be limited in the numbers of times (two) they could qualify for such benefits.

Undoubtedly proposals such as these will sound preposterous to many. Paying girls not to get pregnant? Consider that for years the federal government has paid farmers (price supports) not to produce certain commodities. Consider, too, that if we calculate the costs of teenage pregnancies across a lifetime, including the welfare benefits received not only by mothers but by their children and even their children's children, such a program might actually turn out to be strikingly cost-effective, even if expensive to implement initially ($5650 per teenager and family, if successful). This would seem especially the case if the offspring of girls who defer parenthood until sometime after they turn eighteen end up rearing children who turn out to be productive, tax-generating members of society rather than tax-consuming, welfare-dependent ones.

Future Interests

The actual dollar amounts we suggest may either be more than is necessary or less than is necessary to make it attractive for a sufficient number of girls to remain childless through their high school years. They should be regarded for what they are—mere examples of the kind of graduated incentive system that might be implemented to ensure that it is continually in a teenage girl's and her family's immediate and future interest that she not get pregnant and bear a child. We could even imagine in the case of teenagers who do get pregnant that a parallel program be available, with somewhat less attractive benefits, in the hope of forestalling a second pregnancy.

Cost-Effective

Paying girls not to get pregnant? Consider that for years the federal government has paid farmers (price supports) not to produce certain commodities. Consider, too, that if we calculate the costs of teenage pregnancies across a lifetime, including the welfare benefits received not only by mothers but by their children and even their children's children, such a program might actually turn out to be strikingly cost-effective, even if expensive to implement initially.

Jay Belsky and Patricia Draper, *Society*, March/April 1987.

As a nation we seem to be willing to mortgage our future by generating massive federal deficits to protect our country from foreign threats. Before disregarding a scheme such as the one just proposed, we need to recognize that we are simultaneously generating a demographic deficit in the form of a growing underclass. We further need to recognize that people living in contexts of economic deprivation and without realistic ability to ameliorate their conditions will exhibit reproductive behavior that is adaptive when seen from within, even if fiscally and politically maladaptive when seen from without. Our failure to appreciate these complexities leads to the continual promulgation of stopgap policies and programs which, at best, will enable us only to service our debt, not reduce and eventually pay off the principle. Although we are not convinced that a proposal such as ours would prove effective, we are convinced that a new understanding of the teenage pregnancy problem is required if we are to deal with it effectively. Above all else, this pattern of behavior must be conceived of as a reproductive strategy that fits the ecological niche which all too many impoverished teenagers inhabit. Until the costs and benefits of teenage pregnancy and parenthood change, impoverished teenagers will continue to solve their life-course equations in a strategic manner—by having babies at early ages, by having their kin care for them, and by continuing to have additional offspring in whom their personal investment will be limited.

"Increasing the legitimacy and availability of contraception . . . is likely to result in declining pregnancy rates."

Providing Contraception Lowers the Teenage Pregnancy Rate

Elise F. Jones, et al.

Elise F. Jones was the study director for a project sponsored by the Alan Guttmacher Institute entitled, *Teenage Pregnancy in Industrialized Countries*. The study group researched teenage pregnancy rates in 37 industrialized nations to discover why other nations had much lower teenage pregnancy rates than the US. The study group concluded that other industrialized nations, especially northern European countries, succeed because of their extensive sex education and contraception programs. Jones and her fellow researchers argue that the US should also provide contraceptives, and instructions on their use, to teenagers.

As you read, consider the following questions:

1. In the authors' opinion, why do other nations have much lower teenage pregnancy rates than the US?
2. Why do the authors write that the media's restriction on contraceptive advertising is incongruous?
3. According to the study group members, how have US teenagers inherited the "worst of all possible worlds"?

Elise F. Jones, *Teenage Pregnancy in Industrialized Countries.* New Haven, CT: Yale University Press, 1986. Copyright © 1986 by the Alan Guttmacher Institute.

Does the availability of contraceptives, sex education, and abortion services in the United States encourage sexual promiscuity and thereby account for the higher teenage pregnancy rates in the United States? The finding from the case-study countries suggest that this cannot be the case, since availability is generally greater in countries with lower teenage pregnancy rates.

Teenagers who obtain contraceptives from *any* source are assured of confidentiality of services in Sweden, the Netherlands, and France. It is notable that in England the government went to the House of Lords asking that a previous court decision be reversed which would have required those under age 16 to have parental consent to obtain contraceptive services. The House of Lords law panel, Britian's highest court, agreed with the government that physicians may provide contraceptive services to minors under 16 on their own consent. Conversely, in the United States, the U.S. Justice Department went to court, unsuccessfully, to defend a Department of Health and Human Services regulation that would have *required* that the parents of all teenagers under 18 be notified if their children obtained a prescription contraceptive. (Another branch of government, the U.S. Congress, had rejected a proposal that parental consent or notification be mandated.) . . .

Contraception Can Work

The 37-country study and the individual country studies provide convincing evidence that many widely held beliefs about teenage pregnancy cannot explain the large differences in adolescent pregnancy between the United States and other developed countries: teenagers in these other countries apparently are *not* too immature to use contraceptives consistently and effectively; the availability of welfare services does *not* seem correlated with higher adolescent fertility; teenage pregnancy rates are *lower* in countries where there is *greater* availability of contraceptive and abortion services and of sex education; adolescent sexual activity in the United States is not very different from what it is in countries that have much *lower* teenage pregnancy rates; although the pregnancy rate of American blacks is much higher than that of whites, the white rate is still much higher than the overall teenage pregnancy rates in the other case-study countries; teenage unemployment appears to be at least as serious a problem in all the countries studied as it is in the United States, and American teenagers have more or at least as much schooling as those in most of the countries studied that have lower pregnancy rates. Because the other case-study countries have more extensive public health and welfare benefit systems, however, they do not have so extensive an economically deprived underclass as does the United States. However, the differences in teenage pregnancy rates would probably not be eliminated if socioeconomic status could be controlled.

Clearly, then, it *is* possible to achieve a lower teenage pregnancy rate than that experienced in the United States, and a number of countries with comparable levels of adolescent sexual activity have done so. . . .

Different Tactics

It is important to note that some of the factors associated with low pregnancy rates may differ between countries. For example, school sex education appears to be a much more important factor in Sweden than it is in the other countries; high levels of media exposure to contraceptive information and sex-related topics is more prominent in the Netherlands; condoms are more widely available in England, the Netherlands, and Sweden. Use of the pill by teenagers is most extensive in the Netherlands.

Dan Wasserman. © 1981, Boston Globe. Reprinted by permission of Los Angeles Times Syndicate.

By and large, Sweden has been the most active of the countries studied in developing programs and policies to reduce teenage pregnancy. It is notable that Sweden has *lower* teenage pregnancy rates than have all of the countries examined, except for the Netherlands, although teenagers begin intercourse at earlier ages in Sweden. It is also notable that Sweden is the only one of the countries observed to show a rapid decline in teenage abortion rates in recent years, even after its abortion law was liberalized.

It is also noteworthy that none of the five case-study countries

159

has developed government-sponsored programs designed to discourage teenagers from engaging in sexual relations—even at young ages—a program intervention officially advocated in the United States and rewarded through government subsidies. Although in Sweden committed relationships and responsible sexual behavior are advocated in the school sex education program, most of the countries have preferred to leave such matters to parents and churches. . . .

Contraception in the Schools

Several U.S. communities have instituted school-based health clinics that provide contraceptive services—usually in partnership with health, youth-serving, or other nonprofit agencies. In many cases, parental consent is required to enroll in the health clinics. Contraception, however, is only one of the many health services offered, so that the parent is not specifically informed when contraceptive services or advice are being obtained. The school, which has a continuing relationship with the young person, is in a position to monitor both continuation and any possible medical complications; the student is not lost to follow up because she has dropped out of the clinic.

A complementary approach would be to enhance the current family planning clinic system, by increasing government subsidy, to provide free or low-cost contraceptive services to all teenagers who want them, not just to those from poor families. This is already permissible under federal law and, to some extent, the process has already begun. In 1982, 6 out of 10 contraceptive visits by U.S. teenagers were visits to family planning clinics; and 44 percent of teenagers using the pill, IUD or diaphragm (and 54 percent of those aged 15-17) first obtained their method at a family planning clinic. In point of fact, however, although the high unmet need for family planning services among teenagers in the United States is well documented, federal subsidies in real dollars have declined. . . .

Lack of Sexual Information

Some restrictive laws relating to sexual information have been struck down by the Supreme Court. Sex, nevertheless, is treated far less openly and is surrounded by more ambivalence than it is in most of the countries in the case studies. In virtually all of the countries examined, for example, information about contraception and sexuality is far more available through the media than it is in the United States; condoms are more widely distributed; and advertisements for contraceptives are far more ubiquitous. Shops providing sex-related materials in other countries, such as the Netherlands, are not as sleazy as they are in the United States.

The self-imposed restrictions on contraceptive advertising in the media—especially on television—are incongruous in an era when virtually every other product, including vaginal douches, sanitary napkins, and hemorrhoid preparations, is advertised everywhere and without protest. At least one cable television network in the United States has begun to carry advertisements for spermicides; and sunbathers at New York area beaches during the summer of 1985 could look up and see a popular condom brand advertised via streamers from an airplane. It seems likely that if the restrictions on advertising were lifted, some aggressive manufacturers would develop and promulgate effective advertising campaigns. A recent study sponsored by the U.S. Food and Drug Administration suggests that such advertising may be feasible. Of course, governmental restrictions on advertising prescription drugs except in medical journals also preclude advertising the most widely used reversible contaceptive method—the pill.

Lower Unintended Pregnancies

Sexually active adolescents who practice contraception are less likely to experience an unintended pregnancy than those who do not. Those who use a prescription method (i.e., pills or an IUD) are significantly less likely to become pregnant than those who use nonprescription methods (i.e., condom, foam, rhythm, withdrawal).

Cheryl D. Hayes, *Risking the Future*, 1987.

There is also a need to disseminate more realistic information among the general public and health professionals about the health risks of the pill (which are minimal for teenagers) and about its extensive benefits. Most Americans are badly misinformed on this subject. Although teenagers in other countries have experienced much lower pregnancy rates than U.S. adolescents while using currently available methods, it is probable that the development of new methods more appropriate for teenagers who have episodic sex—such as a once-a-month pill—could greatly reduce pregnancies in the United States, and further reduce them in other countries, too. Yet funds for contraceptive development have declined in real terms in recent years in the United States (the major funder of contraceptive research); and research into a monthly pill is further hampered by governmental restrictions on abortion-related expenditures.

The Worst of All Worlds

In general, American teenagers seem to have inherited the worst of all possible worlds insofar as their exposure to messages about sex are concerned: movies, music, radio, and television tell them that nonmarital sex is romantic, exciting, and titillating; premarital sex and cohabitation are visible ways of life among the adults they see and hear about; their own parents or their parents' friends are likely to be divorced or separated but involved in sexual relationships. Yet, at the same time, young people get the message (now subsidized by the federal government) that good girls should say no. Little that teenagers see or hear about sex informs them about contraception or the consequences of sexual activity. (They are much more likely to hear about abortions than contraception on the daily television soap opera.) Increased exposure to messages about sex has not meant more realistic exposure or exposure to messages about responsible sex. (Nonmarital sex, though it may be irresistible, is branded irresponsible.) Such mixed messages lead to the kind of ambivalence about sex that stifles communication between partners and exposes young people to increased risk of pregnancy, out-of-wedlock births, and abortions. Increasing the legitimacy and availability of contraception and of sex education in its broadest sense is likely to result in declining pregnancy rates, without raising teenage sexual activity rates to any great extent. That has been the experience of most countries of Western Europe, and there is no reason to think it would not also occur in the United States.

"The overall impact of adolescent birth control programs has merely been that of further aggravating the problem of teenage pregnancy."

Providing Contraception Raises the Teenage Pregnancy Rate

Archdiocese of Boston

Many pro-life organizations oppose providing teenagers with sexual information and contraception for fear of condoning premarital sexual activity. In the following viewpoint, a report published by the Catholic Archdiocese of Boston concludes that offering students access to birth control not only sends the wrong message, but actually leads to increased rates of teenage pregnancy. Though teenagers are using birth control more regularly according to the Archdiocese report, increased sexual activity, along with a high rate of contraceptive failure, has caused a rise in teenage pregnancy.

As you read, consider the following questions:

1. According to the report, why have adolescent birth rates declined?
2. If the use of contraceptives is up, how does the Archdiocese account for the increased pregnancy rate?
3. In the report's opinion, what two myths about contraceptives must be dispelled?

Archdiocese of Boston Task Force Report, *Report on School Based Health Clinics*. Brighton, MA: Daughters of St. Paul, 1986. Reprinted with permission.

In assessing the desirability of establishing school based clinics which prescribe or dispense contraceptives in the public schools, it is necessary to take a look at the impact that federally subsidized birth control programs have had on the overall problem of teen pregnancy since its inception in 1970. It might also be worthwhile to consider the following questions in examining the data:

—Has the provision of Adolescent Birth Control services affirmed and promoted a climate of acceptability of adolescent sexual activity to our teens?

—Has this in turn generated/compounded peer pressure on teens to engage in sexual activity?

—Has this in its turn generated a further increase in teenage pregnancy?

The Statistics

The number of teens in federally funded birth control programs increased nearly 400% during the time period between 1971 and 1980 (a period of increasing federal expenditures of family planning services for adolescents); the use of oral contraceptives by teens jumped from 23.8% to 40.6%; between 1971 and 1978 the number of teens who always used contraceptives increased from 10.2% to 30.0%. The same time period also saw a dramatic increase in the percentage of unmarried teens of all age categories who were involved in sexual activity.

The Alan Guttmacher Institute also made note of the increase in sexual activity coinciding with the time period of increased funding for adolescent contraceptive services. "Between 1971 and 1982, the proportion of sexually active unmarried teenagers grew from 28 to 43 percent." The percentage of teenagers who experienced a contraceptive failure jumped from 8.6% to 31.5%; the percent of teens who were pregnant before marriage rose from 8.5% to 16.2%. Abortions to teens younger than 15 increased 256%; abortions to teens between 15 and 19 increased nearly 229%.

The only decline to occur among adolescents was a decline in the percentage of teens who gave birth—59% in 1971 to 49% in 1980; virtually all sources are unanimous in attributing this drop to an increased reliance on abortion.

And during the same time period, there was a sharp increase in the incidence of gonorrhea for adolescent girls—from 761.9/100,000 in 1971 to 1,468.8/100,000 in 1980.

Aggravating the Problem

As evidenced in the data presented, the overall impact of adolescent birth control programs has merely been that of further aggravating the problem of teenage pregnancy. As was stated in the October, 1980 issue of *Family Planning Perspectives*, "more teenagers are using contraceptives and using them more con-

164

sistently than ever before. Yet the number and rate of adolescent pregnancies continues to rise." The pattern presented by the data is extremely clear:

1. Increased availability of birth control services
2. Increased contraceptive use
3. Increased sexual activity
4. Increased contraceptive failure rate
5. Increased teenage pregnancy
6. Increased abortion rate among teenagers
7. Decreased birth rate (attributable to increase in abortion rate)
8. Increase in incidence of sexually transmitted diseases. . . .

In 1970, Dr. Michael Halberstam (*Redbook*) observed, "when the use of contraceptives spreads through a society, one thing that happens is that the age of sexual intercourse and first exposure to unwanted pregnancy drops lower and lower."

[In 1985] the U.S. Centers for Disease Control published some news on teenage pregnancy. Between 1974 and 1980 the pregnancy rate had gone up among sexually active 12- to 14-year-olds with an increased percentage of these pregnancies ending in abortion. Pregnancy rates for the total teenage population had increased, because a much higher proportion of teenagers was sexually active.

More Sexual Activity

Statistics show that flooding the market with birth-control information is likely to increase sexual activity. It may run against what [columnist] Charles Krauthammer calls "intuition," but two studies by Utah researchers show that when the number of teenagers who used family-planning clinics rose from 300,000 to 1.5 million, the teen pregnancy rate increased 19 percent, and births were down only because of abortion.

"Apparently the programs are more effective at convincing teens to avoid birth than to avoid pregnancy," Stan Weed and Joseph Olsen write in *The Wall Street Journal.*

Suzanne Fields, *The Washington Times*, December 23, 1986.

As we have seen, the impact of increased availability of contraceptives (through the same time period as increases in Title X funding) has only served to achieve the following:

- increased adolescent sexual activity
- increased contraceptive use
- increased contraceptive failure
- increased teenage pregnancy
- increased teenage abortion
- increased teenage sexually transmitted diseases

- decrease in the teen birth rate due to increased reliance on abortion

How extensive is the problem of adolescent contraceptive failure? It has been shown that in the time period between 1971 and 1980, the rate of contraceptive failure among teens aged 15-19 rose from 8.6% to 31.5%, representing an overall increase of 266.3%

Contraceptive Failure

In family planning publications, contraceptive failure among teens is a continuous lament.

- Within one year after getting a prescription method from a clinic, one of 8 teenage patients becomes pregnant; within two years, the fraction is nearly one out of four.

  Among black clinic patients, the record is even more dismal; two in ten get pregnant within a year and four in ten do so within two years . . . the fact remains that attending a family planning clinic and obtaining a prescription method there fails to prevent a subsequent premarital pregnancy among a substantial proportion of adolescent patients—especially those who are black.

- For most methods, women under 22 are about twice as likely to experience contraceptive failure as are those 30 and older . . . 12% of those (unmarried teenagers) who always use contraception do so (experience a contraceptive failure) . . . women with annual family incomes under $10,000.00 are two to four times more likely—depending on the contraceptive method chosen—than those with incomes over $15,000.00, to experience a failure.

- The contraceptive failure rate for teens who always use contraception is about 10%. Therefore, hypothetically, if sexual activity among teens reached 100% and the constant use of contraceptives reached 100% we would still have a pregnancy rate of about 10%.

  To state the above figure another way, there are 11 million sexually active teens in the United States; if they all used contraceptives, 100% of the time, we would still have 1.1 million teenage pregnancies annually.

Failing Programs

Unfortunately, most publicized current proposals to stem the tide of unmarried teenage pregnancy center around increasing availability of contraceptives to teens as well as providing counseling and follow-up in their consistent use; in short, advocates plan more of the same, despite the fact that preliminary studies of these types of programs are inconclusive at best and document continued failure at their worst.

According to Ms. Asta Kenney a two-year study of a school based clinic in Kansas City gave disappointing results. From 1983 to 1985 the percentage of students who had used birth control increased sharply, but the percentage who said they had ever been pregnant remained the same.

The Catch

The birth controllers want to distribute their pills, chemicals, and plastic devices to children within the public schools. They tell us of the epidemic of teen pregnancies and how they can help prevent them. It sounds so logical. Prevent the unwanted conceptions by providing contraceptives. What's the catch? They know that 10 out of 100 girls using prescription birth control will become pregnant by the end of one year. Within two years of using prescription birth control, 24% of teenage girls will become pregnant.

Jo Zillhardt, *Citizens for Community Action*, December 1986.

Presumably a first unplanned pregnancy and/or subsequent abortion would provide motivation for clinic clients to consistently and effectively utilize contraceptives, particularly when combined with counseling and follow-up; yet

- according to the January 1-14 [1986] issue of *Ob. Gyn. News*, the Young Parents Program at Children's Hospital in Boston has found that "increased accessibility of birth control after a first pregnancy does not significantly alter the second pregnancy rate in adolescents." Although extended counseling on contraception is an integral part of this program, and 50% of all patients reportedly used oral contraceptives after a first pregnancy, the program showed a repeat pregnancy rate of 17.9% (considered to be compatible with the national average). These results were announced at a Seminar at Harvard Medical School by Dr. Joanne Cox, who is associated with both Harvard and the Young Parents Program. "We were naive to think we could alter the repeat pregnancy rate by making contraceptives more accessible," Dr. Cox is quoted as saying. "For many girls in an economically deprived environment, pregnancy is a way to gain maturity and independence."

No Long-Term Benefit

- The February 15-28 [1986] issue of *Ob. Gyn. News* recounts a similar study at Rutgers Medical School in New Jersey, indicating that "one-on-one counseling of certain abortion patients regarding contraception does not reduce the rate of subsequent unintended pregnancies." Elizabeth King, a counselor at Rutgers, presented this study to a meeting of the

American Public Health Association. Despite "in-depth" counseling sessions to instruct and motivate abortion patients in the use of contraceptives, and follow-up sessions for up to 18 months later, the repeat pregnancy rate was the same as in a control group and none of the counseled patients was using any form of contraception 15 months after the abortion. Ms. King said the failure of this program suggests that "other, poorly understood pressures" are strongly influencing these women, and that research into these factors is needed.

- On May 19, 1985, the *New York Times* reported results from a study conducted in New York, Boston, Phoenix and Riverside (CA) by the Manpower Demonstration Research Corporation. This study, begun in 1980, had received millions of dollars from the U.S. Department of Labor and the Ford Foundation. While increased access to contraceptives was said to have produced "promising" preliminary results in reducing teen pregnancy, later results showed that this reduction was transitory. One year after leaving the program teenagers had the same pregnancy rate as those who had never enrolled.

- In a study published in the March/April 1986 issue of *Family Planning Perspectives*, researchers at the Family Planning Council of Southeastern Pennsylvania report that teenagers given "intensive follow-up" and other "special services" had the same "cumulative 15-month pregnancy rate" (about 13 percent) as the control group which had simply obtained contraceptives at a clinic.

- Dr. Frank Furstenberg and his colleagues pointed out that over a 15-month period, 6 out of 10 young adolescent patients who got a contraceptive at a family planning clinic failed to use it consistently. Since these young women, as a part of a special study, received more than the usual amount of follow-up it is probable that the discontinuation rate among most clinic patients is even higher.

The Underlying Problems

We can only ask ourselves here what are some of the underlying problems which make poor utilization of contraceptives by teens inevitable?

Underlying the problems involved with adolescents and contraceptives are two myths which have permeated society. The first is the popular though mistaken notion perpetuated in presentations to young people that birth control will enable them to engage in sexual activity in perfect "safety," that is, it will completely remove the danger of unplanned pregnancy. The second is the myth that teenage attitudes, circumstances and behavior with regard to contraceptive use will be the same as that of mature adults.

Regarding the first myth, as Malcom Potts, M.D., former medical director of International Planned Parenthood Federation concedes, "it must be emphasized that contraceptives are not to be described as taps which turn on or off the fertilizing power of sperm, or even traffic lights controlling the release of eggs. They all have measurable failure rates and in biological terms, a contraceptive is an agent which extends the length of time taken to conceive."

The same admission was reiterated in the January, 1985 edition of *Issues in Brief*, published by the Alan Guttmacher Institute, and was coupled with a sobering observation regarding effective use of contraceptives by younger women. "No reversible method of contraception is 100% effective, and all methods are less effective in actual use than they are in theory . . . for most methods, women under 22 are about twice as likely to experience contraceptive failure as are those 30 and older."

Adolescent Attitudes

When failure rates for the more commonly advocated forms of contraception for teens are examined, and when the attitudes and behavior of teens regarding contraceptive use is observed, it is easy to see why advocating or affirming teenage sexual activity, as long as contraceptives are utilized, is merely a prescription for further acceleration of the rate of teenage pregnancy.

Regarding the second myth, that adolescent attitudes, circumstances and behavior regarding contraceptive use will be the same as that of a mature adult—it has already been seen that teens function at a developmental level of concrete operational thought, characterized by failure to anticipate future outcomes and haphazard processing of information. Mature adults function at the level of formal operational thought, characterized by anticipating outcomes and associating behavior accordingly. It has also been noted—even by advocates of contraceptive use by adolescents—that "many adolescents fail to use properly and continually a method of birth control" which requires aggressive follow-up; that is, they function at a level of thought significantly different from that of mature adults, even regarding a matter as serious as birth control.

Distinguishing Bias from Reason

The subject of teen pregnancy often generates great emotional responses in people. When dealing with such highly controversial subjects, many will allow their feelings to dominate their powers of reason. Thus, one of the most important critical thinking skills is the ability to distinguish between statements based upon emotion and those based upon a rational consideration of the facts.

The following statements are taken from the viewpoints in this chapter. Consider each statement carefully. *Mark R for any statement you believe is based on reason or a rational consideration of the facts. Mark B for any statement you believe is based on bias, prejudice, or emotion. Mark I for any statement you think is impossible to judge.*

If you are doing this activity as a member of a class or group, compare your answers with those of other class or group members. Be able to explain your answers. You may discover that others will come to different conclusions than you do. Listening to the reasons others present for their answers may give you valuable insights in distinguishing between bias and reason.

R = a statement based upon reason
B = a statement based upon bias
I = a statement impossible to judge

170

1. Teen pregnancy is widely viewed as the very center of the US poverty cycle.

2. The average American teenager has a beer in one hand, a joint in the other, and probably will not escape adolescence without becoming pregnant or impregnating someone.

3. Children having children is a national tragedy.

4. Since teenagers who have children are more likely to become dependent on welfare, they should be encouraged to postpone childbearing.

5. The impact of adolescent birth control programs has been to further aggravate the problem of teenage pregnancy.

6. Teenage pregnancy rates are lower in countries where there is greater availability of contraceptive and abortion services, therefore, the US should employ similar programs.

7. Teenage pregnancy ranks near the top of issues facing black people.

8. The rate of teenage pregnancy has actually decreased during the past two decades because contraceptive use has improved.

9. When left in unsupervised settings, teenagers become pregnant or get involved in drug and alcohol abuse.

10. The children of teenage mothers cannot read, cannot hold jobs, and are at high risk for becoming criminals.

11. It is a myth that teenage contraceptive use will be the same as that of mature adults.

12. Since the Netherlands has lower teenage pregnancy rates than all other industrialized countries, their sex ed programs should be emulated.

13. Like it or not, American adolescents are far more sexually active than they used to be.

14. Studies on teenage sexuality are blown out of proportion by the national media.

15. Young people who fail to finish high school are at a greater risk of becoming parents at an early age.

16. Many adolescents fail to use birth control properly.

Periodical Bibliography

The following articles have been selected to supplement the diverse views presented in this chapter.

Jerry Adler — "A Teen-Pregnancy Epidemic," *Newsweek*, March 25, 1985.

Mary Cantwell — "Pregnancy Prevention," *The New York Times*, June 16, 1986.

Joy Dryfoos — "What the United States Can Learn About Prevention of Teenage Pregnancy from Other Developed Countries," *SIECUS Report*, November 1985.

Jo Ann Gasper — "What Can Government Do To Prevent Teen Pregnancy?" *Christianity Today*, January 17, 1986.

Erica E. Goode — "Telling '80s Kids About Sex," *U.S. News & World Report*, November 16, 1987.

Elisabeth Keiffer — "Five Ways To Prevent Teen Pregnancy," *Family Circle*, May 27, 1986.

Chris Lutes — "The Teenage Pregnancy Epidemic: Is a Cure in Sight?" *Christianity Today*, December 12, 1986.

Susanna McBee — "A Call To Tame the Genie of Teen Sex," *U.S. News & World Report*, December 22, 1986.

Mary McClellan — "Teenage Pregnancy," *Phi Delta Kappan*, June 1987.

Josh McDowell — "Helping Your Children Say No to Promiscuity," *Eternity*, June 1987.

Alvin F. Poussaint — "Expert Suggests Paying Students To Avoid Sex," *Jet*, June 30, 1986.

William Raspberry — "Some Questions on Birth Control and Teen-Agers," *The Washington Post*, October 17, 1986.

Eric Sherman — "Teenage Sex: A Special Report," *Ladies' Home Journal*, October 1986.

Kathleen Teltsch — "Teen-age Pregnancy: Solutions Elusive," *The New York Times*, June 13, 1985.

David Van Biema — "What's Gone Wrong with Teen Sex," *People*, April 13, 1987.

Should Teenagers Make Their Own Sexual Decisions?

Chapter Preface

What role parents should play in the reproductive decisions of their children has become a highly sensitive issue. Many states now allow teens to obtain contraception and abortion services without having to notify their parents. Other states require health clinics to notify the parents of adolescents who request their services.

Many parents argue that because they are held legally and financially responsible for a child until age eighteen, they should be informed and consulted about their childrens' decisions relating to sex, birth control, and abortion. Their opponents assert that justifiable reasons exist for not informing parents of their daughter's pregnancy or their child's need for birth control. They believe that teenagers are mature enough to make their own reproductive decisions. Some health-care experts also maintain that laws regarding parental notification unduly hinder contraceptive and abortion programs, causing harmful delays in providing teens with these services when they are most needed.

At stake in this debate is the question of whether or not the state has a right to interfere in what traditionally has been viewed as a family affair. The following chapter deals with this continuing struggle between parents' rights, children's rights, and the right of the state to intervene in issues concerning public health.

"*Despite the ongoing barrage of guilt-and-fear-provoking propaganda, [teenagers] are defending their right to sexual love.*"

Teenagers Have a Right To Express Their Sexuality

Ellen Willis

The public concern over teenage sexuality has centered mainly on adolescent pregnancy and sexually-transmitted diseases. However, some social commentators have turned the focus of discussion to whether or not teens should be allowed to express their sexuality. In the following viewpoint, Ellen Willis, a senior editor of *The Village Voice*, writes that teenagers have a right to sexual love. Willis maintains that young people must be given access to birth control so they can enjoy sex free from the fear of pregnancy and disease.

As you read, consider the following questions:

1. Why was the author shocked by the reaction to her satirical article?
2. According to Willis, what is the real reason for concern over teenage sexuality?
3. Why does the author believe teenagers should have easy access to birth control?

Ellen Willis, "Teen Lust," *Ms.*, July/August 1987. © Ellen Willis. Reprinted with the author's permission.

In the age of just-say-no, as the focus of moral hysteria shifts from group to group—AIDS sufferers, women who have abortions, pornographers, drug users—one target remains constant: sexually active teenagers. In the public mind, kids who have sex are by definition "promiscuous"; they never have love relationships, let alone monogamous ones. They are responsible for a rampant social disease, "the epidemic of teenage pregnancy." And sometimes, we are warned, the wages of sin are, literally, death: WILD SEX KILLED JENNY blared a New York *Post* headline after 18-year-old Jennifer Levin was strangled during what may or may not have been a sexual encounter in Central Park.

Last fall [1986], a couple of months after the Levin murder, teenage sex panic once again surfaced in New York City. The occasion was the revelation that an on-site health clinic at a city high school had been giving out contraceptives. The Catholic hierarchy and outraged parents and school board members protested. The liberals responsible for the clinic's policy, caught with their secular humanism showing, responded by assuring everyone in sight that they, too, were all for abstinence. They argued that making birth control available does not encourage teenagers to have sex. Did anyone—educator, doctor, birth control provider, social service agency—suggest that teenagers' sexual desires (you know, sexual desires, those sort of primal impulses responsible for humanity's continued existence) are as legitimate as adults'? That making it possible for teenage girls to enjoy sex without fear of pregnancy might actually be a positive thing? Hey, don't all talk at once!

Inconvenience

In the end, the city's Board of Education came up with an ingenious compromise: school clinics could, with parental consent, give out prescriptions for contraceptives, but not the contraceptives themselves. Apparently, allowing teenagers access to birth control is okay in principle, but only if it's made as inconvenient, not to mention as expensive, as possible.

All this pusillanimity drove me to satire, in the form of an article for *The Village Voice* called "Teenage Sex: A Modesty Proposal." In it I denounced society's gutlessness in the face of our Teenage Sex (TS) plague. It was time, I wrote, "to move beyond toothless moralizing . . . time, in short, to make war on TS." I proposed a 12-point program of "benign terrorism," which included indoctrination beginning at birth ("In recent years . . . parents have been told not to slap an infant's hand when it wanders down there, not to tell little kids to stop touching it or you'll cut it off . . . the Victorians had the right idea"); prosecuting TS as child abuse, with jail or compulsory marriage for those convicted; random vaginal testing; the death penalty for contraceptive dealers who sell to minors; castration for a second TS offense.

It wasn't exactly subtle; I was a little worried that maybe I was being too heavy-handed. Then, the day after it appeared, I got a phone call.

A male voice: "I was *outraged* by your article."

"Oh. What outraged you?"

"I thought some of what you had to say made sense, but your *proposals* . . . !"

I didn't know what was more unnerving—that he had taken the whole thing seriously or that he thought it wasn't all bad.

Public Response

Usually, when I write a piece of satire, I get one or two straight-arrow responses; this time I got at least a dozen. Several accused me, in essence, of being over 30 (the sixties live!)—a dried-up, frustrated old bag who was jealous of teenagers and their beautiful young bodies. But some of the letters were not so much polemics as pleas for understanding. "Sex with someone you love, who loves you, with the proper contraception can be the most wonderful feeling in the world—better than drugs," wrote a 19-year-old woman. "Sex isn't dirty; ignorance is."

Guarantee Sexual Rights

'Protection' of young people without a guarantee of their rights to autonomy, privacy, sexual expression and non-ageist relationships is not just meaningless. It is bound to lead to assault upon their minds and emotions, if not their bodies.

Roger Moody, *The Rights of Children*, 1986.

Clearly, something else was going on besides careless reading, humorlessness, or not having heard of Swift. And when I thought about it, I realized what the problem was: I had assumed that my curmudgeonly persona's antisexual rantings were manifestly absurd, and in making that assumption had seriously underestimated the impact of the hysteria I was trying to ridicule.

Rereading the batch of angry letters, most from kids in their teens or just out of them, I saw that not all the writers had taken my article literally. Several knew I was making some kind of joke, only they assumed that it was at their expense—that I was merely emphasizing my hatred of teen sex (or perhaps sex in general) by indulging in a bit of hyperbole. As one woman (whom I'd guess to be in her twenties) put it, getting into what she thought was the spirit of the discussion, "Of course it was humor, wasn't it? I'm sure most mothers out there would go along with prison terms and castration for their licentious teens." Today's teens and post-teens are growing up in a relentlessly mean-spirited time; it's no wonder that some of the kids who read my piece could only see it as one more nasty put-down.

The source of teen sex panic is not really teenage pregnancy. On the contrary, a central aspect of the current panic is fear that if those liberal do-gooders have their way, pregnancy will no longer serve as a self-enforcing deterrent—or failing that, punishment—for "illicit" sex. In recent years the teen pregnancy rate has actually stabilized; the reason it's suddenly an "epidemic" and a social crisis is the rise in pregnancies among *unmarried* teenagers. Under present social conditions, teenage childbearing is at best a serious obstacle to the mother's prospects (assuming she had some to begin with) for an education, economic mobility, and psychic independence, but no one worried much about that so long as the mothers in question were married—they were just embracing (or submitting to, what difference did it make?) women's destiny a little early.

Part of the concern now is economic, since unwed teenage mothers are likely to end up on welfare. But ultimately even proposals to cut off welfare benefits for teen mothers are aimed less at reducing costs than at ending this public subsidy (with its implied tolerance) of "immorality." For sexual conservatives, what matters is maintaining a social and moral norm, however honored in the breach, that condemns sexual activity outside marriage. And whatever else the 1960s sexual revolution may or may not have accomplished, it destroyed that norm for (heterosexual) adults. In the cultural mainstream, sex before marriage is now a taken-for-granted part of growing up, nor does anyone expect the legions of divorced people to be celibate; when bishops and right-wing columnists oppose TV ads for condoms on the grounds that such ads would "encourage premarital sex," they sound laughably out of touch. Clearly, traditionalists' frustration and resentment at having lost this battle are being displaced with special vehemence onto teenagers. Though most teens do in fact have sex, the social and moral norm still dictates that they're not supposed to, at least not till they're 18 or so—and beleagured conservatives are determined to hold the line.

Controlling Women

I say "adults" and "teenagers," but of course I mean "especially women and girls." Neither premarital sex for men nor the age at which they start having it has ever been a serious issue: the basic impulse underlying the anti-teen-sex crusade is maintaining social control over female sexuality. This is most obvious in the debate about teen pregnancy and birth control, but it's also implicit in the rhetoric about teenage "promiscuity"—a label promiscuously applied to women and gay men, rarely to straight men, for whom it's considered natural to sleep with as many women as possible.

Public discussion of the contraceptives-in-the-schools question,

David Wiley for the San Francisco Examiner. Reprinted with permission.

especially in the mass media, has been notably lacking in any sort of feminist perspective. While conservatives make speeches about chastity, and liberals call for pragmatism, one crucial point is lost: as a matter of simple justice, women of any age have a right to the means of controlling their fertility. Without that right, teenage girls cannot hope to have equal freedom and power in their relations with boys or their relation to the world. Beyond this most basic of principles, a feminist approach to the issue of teenage sex would assume that girls ought to have the power to define their needs for sexual pleasure, emotional satisfaction, and (in the age of AIDS) safety—and to resist male pressure for sex on any terms that violate those needs. In short, we need not only contraceptives and sex education in our schools, but feminist consciousness-raising—and a feminist movement.

From this point of view, I take some comfort in the response to my article. The letter writers may have been confused about where I stood, but their anger at the authorities they thought I represented is heartening. These are young people who, despite the ongoing barrage of guilt-and-fear provoking propaganda, are defending their right to sexual love. And half of them are female.

"Teens don't have a right to sex when they can't pay the cost."

Teenagers Should Not Have a Right To Express Their Sexuality

Joseph W. Tkach and Lawrence Wade

Joseph W. Tkach is the publisher of *Plain Truth*, a magazine sponsored by the Worldwide Church of God. Lawrence Wade is a former editor of the conservative newspaper *The Washington Times*. He is now a Washington-based syndicated columnist. In Part I of the following two-part viewpoint, Tkach writes that the problems of teenage pregnancy and sexually-transmitted diseases will not be solved until US society realizes that premarital sex is harmful. In Part II, Wade argues that not only is teenage sex harmful, but wrong. Wade asserts that teenagers have no right to sexual activity if they cannot handle the consequences.

As you read, consider the following questions:

1. According to Tkach, why should society discourage premarital sex?
2. Why does Wade blame the 1960s for today's sexual "decadence"?
3. In Wade's opinion, what are the true rights of adolescents?

I

Healthy attitudes toward sex have probably never been more difficult for young people to acquire than they are today.

Yet, never before has so much information about sex been so readily available to youth. But how much of that information is reliable? And how much of it is accompanied by the guidance necessary to use sex *responsibly*?

The price young people are paying for the irresponsible use of sex is appalling. Some one million teenage girls in the United States become pregnant every year. Perhaps one half have abortions. The other half million give birth to illegitimate children. Countless teenagers suffer from sexually transmitted diseases. How many of these young people will be able to have a happy, productive marriage, not to mention future?

Harmful Attitudes

Society seems to have accepted premarital sex as simply a part of life these days. Supposedly responsible adults often say, "Everybody's doing it. What does it hurt, really? We just need to teach kids how to avoid pregnancy and VD." Somehow, though, sexually active teenagers, who lack self-esteem, just don't seem to be good learners when it comes to avoiding diseases or pregnancy.

One of mankind's age-old shortcomings is that we don't look at the result of our actions. What is the result of premarital sex? How does it affect one's future? How does it affect a future marriage? How does it affect personal relationships? How does it affect one's children?

Society as a whole has compromised with illicit sex to the point that many no longer care. Young people today have to assume that irresponsible sex is OK simply because too many parents, schools, clergy and in government don't have the conviction or determination to guide them responsibly. Where is the leadership and guidance that a young, immature, impressionable mind *needs* in advance on matters that it lacks experience to know for itself?

Serious Consequences

Why should youngsters have to find out the *hard way*—through debilitating STDs, the shock of pregnancy, marriage-wrecking sexual delusions, emotional scars and wasted lives—that premarital and extramarital sex and homosexual activity have serious *consequences*?

The "just say no to sex" concept has been ridiculed as simplistic by some who apparently reason that premarital sex is not in itself wrong. Anyone would admit the above consequences are bad, but the *cause* of those consequences, premarital sex for example, is often considered acceptable, even something to be *expected*. "Look, they're going to do it anyway, so let's at least teach them how to

181

avoid pregnancy," the rhetoric goes. We should ask ourselves, WHY are they "going to do it anyway"?

Is it so inconceivable that educating youngsters about a *better* way, a way that has no debilitating drawbacks, might just help avoid the destructive results of sex outside of marriage? Yet those who call such education "moralizing" wish to push *their* brand of morality on an immature segment of society too inexperienced to defend itself! . . .

Only One Context for Sex

Sex was meant to be experienced between two married people, built upon self-control, discipline, sensitivity, patience, commitment, trust, and faithfulness. When sex is governed by those qualities, it enables a couple to enjoy greater depths of intimacy and togetherness. These building blocks of character lay the foundation for lasting, fulfilling relationships and marriage.

Josh McDowell, *Moody*, September 1987.

Young people *can* be taught the truth. With patient, loving instruction they can be shown the better way. . . .

Do young people respond? They certainly do! Response to [a] *Plain Truth* article "Are You Sure Everybody's Doing It?" showed us that most teens and even young adults deeply appreciate frank, clear guidance that helps them stand up to the strong pressures that could lead to disaster.

Experts correctly point out that lack of self-esteem is a core cause of teenage pregnancy. A sense of rejection and inability to deal with self-doubt make it unlikely a girl will say no to sex with a boy who shows her some attention. Adolescence is a difficult time from any perspective. It is a time when people need support and loving direction from those who should love them most—who should *really* care about their future happiness.

II

Her fragile, young face adorns the cover of *Time* magazine. Her soft, blue eyes gaze innocently forward.

But her belly—swollen and obvious—reveals a harsh reality. "Children Having Children," reads the headline on the cover.

Inside: more girls like her, younger, older, white, black, poor, rich. "Each year more than a million . . . ," reads the story.

Teen pregnancy in America is alarming. *Time* says 80 percent of pregnant girls are unmarried. And the annual cost to us adult taxpayers is an estimated $8.6 billion.

Liberals say what's needed is more sex education. But more of that and less poverty won't solve anything. What's needed is for adults to firmly say that teens have no right to sex in the first place.

Not long ago, parental control of teen-age sex was expected. And unwed teen pregnancies were a minor problem. In 1950, less than 15 percent of teen births were illegitimate. But then came the decadent '60s.

There was a "rights explosion." Much of it was needed, such as civil rights for minorities and women. But much of it went too far with the so-called rights of children.

Organizations such as Planned Parenthood Federation of America Inc. shoved parents and churches aside and assumed their roles. Frisky teens can't resist sex, they insisted, so give them tools with which to do it.

At the same time, family and religious beliefs were mocked. The stigma attached to "bad girls" was sanitized, despite the fact that the admittedly sexist stigma worked.

In the Washington-area today, unwed girls with babies tote them to school day-care centers—proudly—like they once displayed new stereos or daddy's T-Bird convertible.

Today Planned Parenthood derides American morality. Says President Faye Wattleton, "We are still very much governed by our puritanical heritage." But that puritanism kept young people from ruining their lives with unplanned pregnancies.

Parents' Rights

Parents have acquiesced their rights to liberals. The result has been an explosion of promiscuity: in 1982 about 47 percent of teenage girls—4.5 million—were no longer virgins.

Despite hundreds of millions spent on birth control, we have a nation of babies raising babies, and a future of welfare bums, junkies, and hoodlums.

Uncle Sam is a failure as a father. And his failure isn't due to too little money spent on counselors, clinics, or condoms.

If ignorance was the answer, why wasn't the teen pregnancy rate for unwed mothers higher in the past?

Why wasn't it a problem in 1950 when 30 percent of *all* Americans lived in poverty?

Sure, life has changed.

In 1955, juice was sold by Donald Duck rather than by hip-shaking Lolitas and Romeos flashing goo-goo eyes at each other. But the major change has been in families. How often did your folks shrug, "They're going to do it anyway." These kids' folks are too busy meeting BMW payments to control their teens' behavior.

I believe what adults do in private is their business. You and I may not like homosexuality, for example, but ultimately it's a matter between individuals and their Maker.

What sexually active teens do is *all* our business. Teens don't have a right to sex when they can't pay the cost. It's like a right to drive whether or not you can afford insurance.

Children *do* have some rights.

They've the right to be raised by caring adults. They've the right not to be abused, physically or mentally.

They've the right not to have their parents' moral and spiritual teachings blasphemed in public schools by sex education and so-called situational ethics.

An Illegal Activity

The time has come for the American public to demand that the public schools teach children to say NO to fornication, as well as NO to drugs and NO to alcohol. Those are all illegal for children, anyway. Any other instruction in the public schools about these three subjects is tantamount to leading children down the primrose path of behavior that is unhealthy.

Phyllis Schlafly, *Manchester Union Leader,* February 3, 1987.

But children have no right to sex at the drop of their Calvin Kleins, and not just because they can't pay for the consequences. They've no right because a power higher than Faye Wattleton gave their parents dominion over their activities.

And if parents can't enforce that right, then government should make them do so. In Wisconsin, a law makes grandparents of babies born to unwed mothers financially responsible.

Watch how fast the teen pregnancy rate falls in that state.

Better yet: bring back "shotgun weddings."

"[Parental notice laws] ensure that those who become pregnant are more likely to obtain the advice and support of their parents."

Parental Notification Laws Are Beneficial

Maura K. Quinlan

Supporters of parental notification laws maintain that an abortion is often the only medical procedure a minor can receive without parental permission. Many parents would like to see laws created which include them in the decision-making process. In the following viewpoint, Maura K. Quinlan, chief staff counsel for Americans United for Life, writes that parental notification laws open communication between pregnant teens and their parents. Quinlan believes that teenagers need their parents' support when deciding how to resolve their pregnancies.

As you read, consider the following questions:

1. What three reasons does the author list for supporting parental notification laws?
2. According to Quinlan, why is a teenager's attempt to hide her pregnancy from her parents often harmful?
3. Why does the author believe parental notification laws reduce teen pregnancy?

Maura K. Quinlan, "Parental Notice Requirements and Young Pregnant Women," a position paper, November 17, 1987. Reprinted with the author's permission.

Young women who find themselves unintentionally pregnant experience, perhaps, no greater trauma or stress in their lives. As often has been said, there is no such thing as being "just a little bit" pregnant. The sudden knowledge that you carry within you a new, developing baby who is totally dependent upon you is staggering—even to many adult women. Once pregnant, there are only two options: 1) carry the unborn baby to term, allowing him or her to continue developing and growing, or 2) obtain an abortion which takes the life of the unborn child and prevents his or her continued growth and development. . . .

Once pregnant, the decision of how that pregnancy will end—in birth or by abortion—is, perhaps, the most important kind of decision that a young person will ever have to make. That decision should not be made by a young pregnant woman, who is alone, confused and under tremendous emotional stress. Nor should it be made by abortion clinic personnel who have a financial stake in the outcome of the decision and counsel in favor of a "quick and easy" abortion that will net them hundreds of dollars. The decision should be made in consultation with the young woman's parents and family, who know her, love her and care about her well-being and long-term happiness. And, even then, it should not be made hastily without careful evaluation of the alternative outcomes and choices available.

Benefits of Parental Notice

To help achieve this end, several states have enacted laws requiring that parents be notified prior to the performance of an abortion on a young woman. These laws typically provide for an exception to parental notice for extreme cases where physical abuse or other harm might be inflicted upon the pregnant young woman by her parents.

There are at least three very good reasons for passing laws requiring parental notice as was done in Minnesota. First, parents generally have the best interests of their children at heart, and will give them needed advice and support during a most stressful time. Second, parents frequently find out about an abortion sooner or later. Failure to notify them before the abortion, when they can discuss the proper course of action with their daughter, may cause additional family tension and endanger a young woman's life or health. Finally, the existence of such laws appears to reduce the incidence of pregnancy for young women in their teens, thereby eliminating the need for making any life-changing decision regarding pregnancy outcome.

Support from Parents

Many young people misjudge the reactions of their parents, believing that their response to news of pregnancy will be harsher than it is. In the absence of a law requiring parental notice, these young people will avoid notifying their parents and will be deprived of their best support system and advice-givers.

It is true that most parents will be disappointed and many will be angry, initially. However, most parents, because they love their children and care deeply about their well-being, will attempt to help them through this most difficult time and will prove, ultimately, to be very supportive.

The young woman who does not seek the guidance and support of her parents is more likely to make a less considered decision and is easily preyed upon in her vulnerable condition. Without discussing her options with her parents, it is impossible to be certain of the amount of support that will be available to her. Certainly, no irreversible decision of the magnitude of the decision to abort an unborn child should be made without all of the necessary information.

The Ultimate Say

Abortion advocates note that many teenagers don't get along with their parents, and that notification statutes encourage them to delay having abortions or to resort to back-alley butchers. Maybe so in extreme cases. But unless parents are found guilty of child abuse, the presumption has to be that they have more say in the life of their children than does the state, the abortionist, the ACLU [American Civil Liberties Union], or the director of the local Planned Parenthood clinic.

The Washington Times, February 6, 1987.

In addition, most young women obtain abortions at abortion clinics where little if any counseling takes place. Therefore they are left adrift to deal with their problem on their own. The doctor who performs the abortion rarely sees the patient before proceeding with the abortion. Abortion clinic personnel, who do not know the troubled young woman who is seeking advice, speak with her only a few minutes (frequently in a group, not one-on-one). They cannot know her strengths and weaknesses because they have virtually no information on which to base their advice. And, since abortion clinics have a financial interest in selling abortions, it is inevitable that any information they give will be biased in favor of abortion.

Unnecessary Pain

Frequently, the decision not to inform one's parents is based on a desire to prevent them from ever knowing about the pregnancy and being hurt and disappointed. As most young people know, however, no matter how secret something is kept, parents have a way of finding out about it sooner or later. One easy way for parents to find out about an abortion can be seen from a case in California. A fourteen year old was taken for an abortion by her teacher, the teacher having sent a note home to her mother saying that she was babysitting for the teacher. The abortion was performed without the mother's knowledge, but complications from the abortion arose a few days after and immediate medical attention was necessary. Since parental consent is generally necessary for any child to obtain surgical care, the mother was notified and told of the reason for the medical treatment.

However hurt parents may be at finding out about a pregnancy, they will be doubly hurt by finding out that their daughter was not only pregnant but obtained an abortion without involving them in the decision-making process or seeking their advice and support. Thus, in attempting to avoid hurting the parents, the daughter will have hurt them even more if and when they find out about the abortion.

Moreover, knowing that she has deceived her parents and having alienated herself from her best support system, the young woman may be more hesitant to obtain necessary medical treatment for abortion complications. Failure to obtain necessary emergency medical care could seriously endanger a young woman's life and health.

Reduction in Pregnancy

The choices involved in determining the outcome of a young woman's pregnancy are very difficult. It is obvious that the most desirable course of action is to avoid pregnancy in the first place. It appears that the very existence of parental notice laws reduces the incidence of pregnancy for young women in their teens. Between 1980 (the last full year prior to enforcement of the Minnesota parental notice law) and 1984 (the last year for which statistics are available from the Minnesota Department of Health), the number of pregnancies (abortion plus births) for Minnesota teens under age 18 dropped 30.1% and the pregnancy rate decreased 20.9%

Law, in general, is a teacher. It sets guidelines and standards and thereby helps to shape and direct behavior. A law which clearly establishes that parents will be notified prior to an abortion upon their daughter will have an affect on the behavior of young people. An awareness of the certainty of the consequences of one's actions tends to make one more careful in acting. If a young woman knows for certain that her parents will be notified of her pregnancy (not just that they might find out), she may be more likely to be more cautious about preventing pregnancy in the first place. For example, in response to a question from a judge regarding whether she had attempted to prevent pregnancy, one young woman indicated that she had not, since she thought that she could easily obtain an abortion without her parents learning about it. Presumably, this young woman would have used preventive measures or avoided sexual activity had she known that her parents would be notified in the event she became pregnant and sought an abortion.

Also, some young women are pressured into engaging in sexual activity and have no ready excuse for refusing to do so. Young women today are deprived of, perhaps, the most used excuse prior to the legalization of abortion—"I might get pregnant and have a baby." They also cannot rely, as prior generations of young women were able to, on the parental backstop—"My parents would find out." Thus, the legalization of abortion and the elimination of parents from the picture has made growing up much more difficult for today's young woman. Now, she is confronted with the notion that there is nothing to lose from engaging in early sexual activity since she can always get an abortion without her parents ever knowing about it if she gets pregnant.

Parental notice laws afford those young women who are not yet assertive enough to object to being pressured into sexual activity, an easy excuse for avoiding it.

The Child's Best Interest

The Illinois Parental Notice of Abortion Act provides a mandatory waiting period—24 hours—for a dependent, immature minor seeking abortion after notice of her intention is given to her parents. . . . During the waiting period, parents may consult with and advise their daughter about the intended abortion and its consequences. Presumptively, parents will act out of genuine concern to advance the welfare of their child. . . . Whether the parents agree or disagree with her decision is beside the point. At least the family is entitled to the time and the private space for a discussion.

US Catholic Conference, *Origins*, January 8, 1987.

Parental notice laws serve many beneficial purposes. While they may not benefit every young woman, laws are made to benefit the majority of those they cover. The vast majority of young women will be benefited by such laws. Not only to they ensure that those who become pregnant are more likely to obtain the advice and support of their parents during a most stressful time, but they also appear to impact significantly upon the number of young women who will become pregnant.

"Parental consent and notification laws are not motivated by a desire to help teenagers."

Parental Notification Laws Are Harmful

Susan Blank

Some states have enacted parental notification laws for pregnant teenagers under age 18 who want to have an abortion. This controversial law requires abortion clinics to contact a pregnant minor's parents before an abortion can be performed. In the following viewpoint Susan Blank, a writer for the American Civil Liberties Union publication *Civil Liberties*, states that notification laws make pregnancy decisions more traumatic than necessary. Minors, Blank argues, often have good reason for not notifying parents of an impending abortion.

As you read, consider the following questions:

1. Why does Blank believe that parental notification laws make abortion more difficult?
2. In the author's opinion, why do pregnant minors often keep their abortion decision secret?
3. According to Blank, how do parental notification laws affect teens' decisions concerning pregnancy?

Susan Blank, "The Case Against Parental Notice Laws," *Civil Liberties*, Winter 1987. Reprinted with permission.

On the face of it, the law might have looked like a reasonable compromise—a way of satisfying those who think a minor must get parental permission for an abortion, without destroying the principle that she should be free to keep the decision confidential. If a teenager younger than 18 was unwilling to tell her parents that she wanted to terminate her pregnancy, a 1981 Minnesota statute gave her another option: Using what is known as a "judical bypass mechanism," she could go to court and have a judge decide whether an abortion was in her best interest.

But after a successful ACLU [American Civil Liberties Union] challenge to the law in U.S. district court, Minnesotans who might have initially dismissed qualms about the law could have little doubt that its consequences had been disastrous for teens in their state. These consequences are now documented by the ACLU's Reproductive Freedom Project in a report entitled *Parental Notice Laws: Their Catastrophic Impact on Teenagers' Right to Abortion*.

An Obstacle Course

For a pregnant teenager, a judicial bypass law sets up an obstacle course—and only when she reaches the finish line is she free to exercise the right to terminate her pregnancy. Negotiating the legal maze can mean sneaking out of school. It can involve finding a court, often hours distant from her hometown and not open on weekends, willing to hear her case. It entails compromising her privacy—the typical Minnesota minor who wound her way through the court process faced as many as 23 strangers who knew her first name and her situation. Frequently it means that when the teen finally secures an abortion the procedure has become both riskier and more costly.

The record in the Minnesota case, *Hodgson* v. *State of Minnesota*, speaks volumes about the emotional costs the judicial bypass procedure exacted from young women already under the stress of an unwanted pregnancy. Some teens reacted to the shame of having to appear in court by "trying to become invisible" staring at the floor or facing the walls. Some became ill and vomited. Many said they dreaded the court appearance more than the abortion. In the opinion of numerous judges, health professionals and court-appointed guardians, the legislation produced no countervailing benefits whatsoever.

With only a miniscule proportion of abortion requests denied, the law apparently never even encouraged serious judicial decision making. One state court judge who had heard over 1,000 parental notification petitions described his relationship to the typical abortion request as "just like putting my seal and stamp on it."

While the *Hodgson* case is an important victory in the struggle to allow women to make their own reproductive choices, the issue

191

of whether states can establish special notification procedures for pregnant minors has not been laid to rest. The major stumbling block is the U.S. Supreme Court. In a divided 1979 opinion, four justices suggested that an administrative or judicial bypass mechanism might make it constitutional for states to require minors to notify or get consent from their parents for abortions.

In the Minnesota case, District Court Judge Alsop rejected the parental notice statute on narrow grounds, ruling, for example, that the law was unconstitutional because it required a teen to notify not just one but both parents to avoid going to court. But based on what he had heard in his courtroom. Alsop also included broader objections to the law in his written opinion. "Five weeks of trial," he concluded, "have produced no factual basis upon which the court can find that the statute on the whole furthers in any meaningful way the state's interest in protecting pregnant minors or assuring family integrity."

Negative Impact

When Minnesota's parental-consent bill was struck down, the evidence at the trial overwhelmingly demonstrated that the state's five-year experiment with lives of pregnant minors was an unqualified failure. The state was unable to show any support for its argument that this law protected pregnant minors or promoted family unity. And the state could not dispel the dramatic reality that in the five years during which parental consent was required, Minnesota's teen birthrate soared, the number of dangerous second-trimester abortions for minors increased, and the number of doctors willing to get involved in providing abortions to minors decreased.

Carol Sobel and Jo Ellen Pasman, *Los Angeles Times*, September 29, 1987.

Drawing together key elements of the *Hodgson* testimony with information and analysis from other sources, the ACLU's report makes the following points against parental consent laws:

• *Parental consent and notification laws are not motivated by a desire to help teenagers.*

All such laws passed in the last 13 years have been drafted by anti-choice groups. In Minnesota, for example, the only group that publicly expressed an interest in the legislation was Minnesota Citizens Concerned for Life, which supported the law because it would "save lives."

• *Most teenagers voluntarily tell parents about a pregnancy or proposed abortion. When they keep this information confidential, it is most often because they have good reason to do so.*

National surveys confirm that over half of minors who obtain clinic abortions have already informed a parent of their choice.

The younger the teen, the more likely is her parent to know. The state court judges who testified at the *Hodgson* trial, themselves experts in evaluating the credibility of witnesses, agreed that minors who chose not to disclose their pregnancies to their parents had well founded fears about the suffering this information could unleash.

As one teen described the family powderkeg that was likely to be ignited with the news of her pregnancy: "My mother . . . has a documented past of severe mental illness. She has been hospitalized several times during my lifetime. . . . My father has a violent temper. His inital reaction would have been violent and angry and he probably would have hit me." One expert witness characterized the effects that can be expected when a family with an abusive father is notified of a teen pregnancy as "showing a red cape to a bull."

Rising Birthrates

• *Consent laws deter minors from obtaining abortions and cause more of them to carry to term.*

An Alan Guttmacher Institute survey of 2,400 minors who were patients at family planning or abortion clinics revealed that 44 percent of them had not informed their parents of their decisions to terminate their pregnancies. Of that group 23 percent said that if they had been required to do so, they would have dropped their plans for abortions.

Between 1980 and 1984, a period encompassing the implementation of the Minnesota law, the birthrate for 15- to 17-year-olds in Minneapolis rose 38 percent. Meanwhile, the rate for 18- and 19-year-olds, a group untouched by the requirement, grew by only .3 percent.

• *It is by no means easy for a teen to get her day in court to request a judicial bypass. The result is a two-tiered system, with advantaged teens more apt to follow through on the procedure, and other less-fortunate adolescents likely to be deterred from seeking abortions.*

In Minnesota, as in many states, some courts are open only a few days a week, and some counties have no full-time judge. Many judges refused to hear the cases at all. Given court backlogs and busy schedules, many minors had to wait days and even weeks before they could proceed with an abortion.

Not surprisingly, the teens most likely to persist were those with the most resources. All of the 16- and 17-year-old minors who went through Minnesota's court bypass procedure in 1983 were described as "white, middle class, well dressed, educated, and mature."

• *A teen who must use pre-counseling abortion sessions to cope with the aftermath of a court appearance is unable to focus properly on the issues associated with the abortion itself.*

Minnesota health professionals who expected to offer minors an orderly, reassuring experience of information and counseling, often found themselves confronted with tense and angry teens who had just spent their mornings under interrogation by strangers in the intimidating and chaotic world of the courthouse. Helping teens overcome the effects of that experience intruded on the normal pre-abortion orientation and counseling discussions.

• *In a medical situation in which prompt action is imperative, the delays entailed by judicial bypass laws transform an unusually safe procedure into a more dangerous one.*

Abortion is one of the least risky surgical procedures that doctors perform. But timing is critical. A leading reproductive specialist concludes that "delay has the largest single effect on the risk to teenagers of complications and death from abortion."

No Benefit

While advocates of parental consent laws support the concept in the name of family unity, enhanced communication between parents and their childen, protection of young adolescents who are unable to make mature decisions, and a reduction in the rate of abortion among them, there is little evidence that this law is having those effects.

Virginia G. Cartoof and Lorraine V. Klerman, *American Journal of Public Health*, April 1986.

Alarmed by the possibility that judicial bypass requirements could push teens into second trimester abortions, the National Academy of Science specifically recommended that such laws not be enacted. The academy has good grounds for its concern: The Minnesota law increased the percentage of minors who sought out second-trimester abortions by more than 25 percent.

Reproductive Free Choice

The *Hodgson* decision spotlights the inconsistencies between judicial bypass mechanisms and guarantees of reproductive free choice. "This case," says Janet Benshoof, director of the ACLU's Reproductive Freedom Project, "is a vindication of the rights of minors who have been needlessly suffering under a system designed to make political points at the expense of young women's constitutional rights."

"If a pregnant teenager's parents are ultimately responsible for . . . her baby, then give those parents the right to decide whether or not the teenager keeps her baby."

Parents Should Control Teenage Reproductive Decisions

Ronnie Gunnerson

Parents of teenage mothers are legally responsible for their daughter and grandchild until the daughter becomes 18. Many people believe this responsibility is unjust because parents are often powerless to decide whether or not their daughter keeps the child. In the following viewpoint, Ronnie Gunnerson, an editor for North American Publishing Company and a mother, writes of the emotional trauma created by her daughter's pregnancy. Gunnerson was dismayed by what she saw as her lack of legal rights to help make a decision that would ultimately affect her and her family.

As you read, consider the following questions:

1. According to the author, how are parents the victims of teenage pregnancy?
2. In Gunnerson's opinion, why was her daughter's pregnancy more difficult for her than for her daughter?
3. Why does the author believe parents should have a right to dictate their children's reproductive decisions?

"What's a parent to do?" is the punch line to many a joke on the perils of raising children. But what a parent does when a teenager gets pregnant is far from a joke; it's a soul-searching, heart-wrenching condition with responses as diverse as the families affected.

In an era besotted with concern for both the emotional and social welfare of teenage mothers and their babies, anger seems to be forbidden. Yet how many parents can deny anger when circumstances over which they have no control force them into untenable situations?

And untenable they are. What I discovered after my 16-year-old stepdaughter became pregnant shocked me. Parents have no rights. We cannot insist on either adoption or abortion. The choice belongs to the teenage mother, who is still a child herself and far from capable of understanding the lifelong ramifications of whatever choice she makes.

Parents Pay the Price

On the other hand, homes for unwed mothers, at least the two we checked in Los Angeles, where we live, will house the teenager at no cost to the family, but they will not admit her unless her parents sign a statement agreeing to pick up both her and her baby from a designated maternity hospital. Parents may sit out the pregnancy, if they so desire, but when all is said and done, they're stuck with both mother and baby whether they like it or not.

In essence, then, the pregnant teenager can choose whether or not to have her baby and whether or not to keep it. The parents, who have the legal responsibility for both the teenage mother and her child, have no say in the matter. The costs of a teenage pregnancy are high; yes, the teenager's life is forever changed by her untimely pregnancy and childbirth. But life is forever changed for the rest of her family as well, and I am tired of sympathy for teen "victims" from do-gooders who haven't walked even a yard in my shoes.

Are Parents To Blame?

What about the victimized parents? Are we supposed to accept the popular notion that we failed this child and that therefore we are to blame for her lack of either scruples or responsibility? Not when we spend endless hours and thousands of dollars in therapy trying to help a girl whose behavior has been rebellious since the age of 13. Not when we have heart-to-heart talks until the wee hours of the morning which we learn are the butt of jokes between her and her friends. And not when we continually trust her only to think afterward that she's repeatedly lied to us about everything there is to lie about.

Yes, the teenager is a victim—a victim of illusions fostered by a society that gives her the right to decide whether or not to have an illegitimate baby, no matter what her parents say. Many believe that feelings of rejection motivate girls to have babies; they want human beings of their own to love and be loved by. I wouldn't argue, but another motive may be at work, too; the ultimate rebellion. Parents are forced to cope with feelings more devastating than adolescent confusion. I'm not talking about what-will-the-Joneses-think concerns. I mean gut-gripping questions that brutally undermine adults' hard-won self-confidence.

The Guilt of Parenting

We can all write off to immaturity mistakes made in adolescence. To what do we attribute our perceived parental failures at 40 or 50? Even as I proclaim our innocence in my stepdaughter's folly, I will carry to my grave, as I know my husband will, the nagging fear that we could have prevented it *if only* we'd been *better* parents.

And I will carry forevermore the sad realization that I'm not the compassionate person I'd tried so hard to be and actually thought I was. My reaction to my stepdaughter's pregnancy horrified me. I was consumed with hatred and anger. Any concern I felt for her was overridden by the feeling that I'd been had. I'd befriended this child, housed her and counseled her for years, and what did I get in return? Not knowing her whereabouts that culminated in her getting pregnant with a boy we didn't even know. At first I felt like a fool. When I discovered how blatantly society's rules favor the rule breaker, I felt like a raving maniac.

A Return to Parental Control

Sex problems are not going to be solved in isolation. A restoration of parental authority over adolescents is essential, even if this means creating unemployment among "experts." It would also mean scrapping many of the legal reforms of the past generation which have facilitated irresponsibility. (For example, abortion is the only medical operation that can be performed on a minor legally without parental knowledge or consent.)

Thomas Sowell, *The Union Leader*, October 21, 1987.

It took more hours of counseling for me to accept my anger than it did for my stepdaughter to deal with her pregnancy. But then, she had the support of a teenage subculture that reveres motherhood among its own and of a news-media culture that fusses and frets over adolescent mothers. Few ears were willing to hear what my husband and I were feeling. While I can't speak for my husband, I can say that a year after the baby's birth, he still turns to ice when his daughter is around. Smitten as he is with his first grandchild, he hasn't forgotten that the joy at the boy's birth was overshadowed by resentment and rage.

Fortunately, my stepdaughter recently married a young man who loves her son as his own, although he is not the father. Together, the three of them are a family who, like many a young family, are struggling to make ends meet. Neither my stepdaughter nor her husband has yet finished high school, but they are not a drain on society as many teenage parents are. She and her husband seem to be honest, hard workers, and I really think they will make it. Their story will have a happy ending.

My stepdaughter says she can't even understand the person she used to be, and I believe her. Unfortunately, the minds of adults are not quite as malleable as those of constantly changing adolescents. My husband and I haven't forgotten—and I'm not quite sure we've forgiven—either our daughter or ourselves. We're still writing the ending to our own story, and I believe it's time for society to write an ending of its own. If a pregnant teenager's parents are ultimately responsible for the teenager and her baby, then give those parents the right to decide whether or not the teenager keeps her baby. Taking the decision away from the teen mother would eliminate her power over her parents and could give pause to her reckless pursuit of the ''in'' thing.

"The bottom line is that you are in charge of your sexuality; the choices are yours."

Teenagers Should Make Their Own Reproductive Decisions

Nancy J. Kolodny, Robert C. Kolodny, and Thomas E. Bratter

Nancy J. Kolodny, Robert C. Kolodny, and Thomas E. Bratter are experts in psychiatry and medicine who previously authored *How to Survive Your Adolescent's Adolescence*. In the following viewpoint, the authors advise pregnant teens to methodically research the options of how to resolve their pregnancies. The viewpoint, written to teenagers, expresses the authors' belief that the pregnant teen is the only person who should make the decision about the future of her pregnancy.

As you read, consider the following questions:

1. According to the authors, what can be done to avoid a panicked reaction to pregnancy?
2. In the authors' opinion, why might it be hard to turn to parents for support?
3. How do the authors suggest teens research their decision?

The prospect of having to admit, "I'm pregnant," or "I got a girl pregnant" can be devastating. Sometimes it throws you into a state of shock to such an extent that you may panic and do things that aren't logical. You may react and make decisions based on the belief that there really is a pregnancy without first checking to see if that's actually true.

> I spent the last two months of my junior year thinking I was pregnant. I walked around like a zombie. I cried at the drop of a hat. My boyfriend and I made plans to run away. I was sure I felt nauseous in the mornings. I lost my appetite and then it came back like I was a starving person. I was tired all the time. It never dawned on me that something else might be wrong with me and I was too scared to go to a doctor. I wasn't pregnant and I ruined two whole months of my life.
>
> *Karen K., age sixteen*

A much more extreme example of this is illustrated by the case of Cathleen Crowley Webb, who accused Gary Dotson of raping her in July, 1977. He was tried, convicted, and sentenced to twenty-five to fifty years in prison and had served six years when, in March 1985, Mrs. Webb came forward and admitted she lied about the rape (thus gaining Dotson's release).

> I concocted the whole story . . . because I had sex with my boyfriend, and I thought I might be pregnant and didn't want to get into trouble with my foster parents.
>
> *Cathleen Crowley Webb*
> *(People Magazine, April 28, 1985, p. 36.)*

To an outside observer these two situations seem unbelievable. They're not. Panic reactions happen when they don't need to. . . .

What To Do

See an obstetrician/gynecologist or a health care professional who specializes in caring for pregnant women (nurse midwives, doctors and nurses who work at women's health centers). Making an appointment for a check-up is easy; keeping the appointment may be harder, especially if you are scared. You may be worried that the doctor or nurse will notify your parents and you may not want your parents to find out just yet. If that is what's preventing you from getting health care, you have the right to request that any information you tell the health care professional is to remain *confidential*—a private matter between you and the person examining you. Most doctors will respect such a request. . . .

Confide in your parents or guardian. Ideally, if you think you're pregnant you'll be able to tell your parents and ask for their advice and help—financial and emotional. But if you can't, don't let that stop you from assuming responsibility for getting medical attention for yourself.

In this day and age, there is absolutely no reason why anyone should go around guessing about a pregnancy. The earlier you can find out whether or not you are pregnant, the better the outcome either way. If you're not, you'll save yourself lots of turmoil and anxiety. If you are, you'll be in a position to know how to protect your health and decide what to do next.

Parental Reaction

Reactions to the news of an unplanned pregnancy tend to be predictable for parents and teenagers alike, and occur in a series of stages. The first stage is usually denial. On the parent side, this takes the form of the "It can't be" syndrome. You may hear, "it can't be because . . ."

". . . I taught my son to be respectful where girls are concerned."

". . . my son would *never* take advantage of a girl that way."

". . . I gave my son a box of condoms for his fifteenth birthday along with a book about sex."

". . . my daughter is an assistant teacher at Sunday school."

". . . my daughter has plans to go to college next fall. She would never do this to herself."

". . . my daughter is too smart to let that happen to her."

". . . my daughter told me none of the kids in her group approved of premarital sex."

Parental Incompetance

To assume that a parent is always the best consultant in the awful business of deciding what to do about an unwanted pregnancy is to be sadly naive about the nature of parent-child relationships today. Every shred of information shows that parents either refuse or cannot handle the embarrassment and anxiety of even so much as a little at-home sex education. Why would anyone believe that these same parents would be able to offer sound counsel once their child was pregnant? How many parents function as parents at all?

Mary Anne Dolan, *Los Angeles Times*, February 27, 1987.

There are endless variations of "It can't be" and parents say them in an attempt to establish logical, believable reasons why their sons or daughters would never get into a situation like that. . . .

The next stage for parents can be shock and anger (with a large dose of guilt). It was this kind of reaction Cathleen Crowley Webb was herself afraid of when she made up the rape story. Parents may say things like,

"I'm going to kill you and (her, him)."

"Look what you've done to our family." ("How could you do this to me?" is a variation.) "What will the neighbors say?"

"Get out of my sight. I'm not going to support someone who sleeps around."

"You'll pay for this. You've lost every privilege you've ever had."

If these are their reactions, try to understand that your parents are being so emotional that they're temporarily incapable of dealing reasonably with the stress of the situation. Unplanned pregnancies throw parents into a state of shock too, and their early reactions may show they're just as scared as you may be.

> When I found out that Marina was pregnant, all I could think of was that she let me down. Those years of teaching her moral values just flew out the window—it was like a slap in the face. Honestly, for days I couldn't consider her side of it. I felt as if she did it to hurt me personally. I told her I'd arrange for an abortion, I'd pay for it, and we'd never mention it to anyone. I didn't ask her if she wanted one. I worried what her uncle would say (her father's dead). I tried to take control. Finally, she ran away. It was only for two days but it woke me up. We could talk after that.
>
> *Mrs. S., age fifty-two*

Anger often masks parents' underlying feelings of pain and confusion. It can also make it seem like they won't be there to help you, and it can drive a wedge between them and you just at the moment you need them most.

> I tried to tell my mom it had nothing to do with her. I really loved the guy I was dating and was hoping to marry him. He usually used condoms but the night I got pregnant he was out of them and I thought I was too close to getting my period to be able to get pregnant. We usually were responsible and careful about having sex. My mom called me a whore. I told her I was sorry, and she kept getting angrier and angrier. That's why I left. I thought she'd physically hurt me she was so mad.
>
> *Marina S., age sixteen (Mrs. S.'s daughter)*

If you're pregnant and caught up in this web of miscommunication with your parents, you might tell them, "I'm sorry," "I didn't mean to hurt you," or "I didn't mean to do it," but those answers don't really help solve the question of what to do next.

The third stage is accepting the pregnancy as a fact of life, abandoning the arguments, blame, and guilt, and turning the feeling of "this can't be happening to me" into one of "this *is* happening to me and I can deal with it."

You Make the Choice

When we say "you" we mean *you*. Early in a pregnancy you must decide what you think it best for you. We don't mean what you think your parents think is best, or your boyfriend, or anyone else. First, examine the situation only from a selfish perspective. Assume responsibility for what has happened and begin to rely on yourself for solutions.

How should you begin? Approach the problem the way you would deal with a school assignment about which you have absolutely no information. Clear your mind of any pre-existing ideas and start from scratch. Be an investigative reporter. Do some library research: read some books or articles about pregnancy, childbirth, abortion, and child care. If you're reading this now, you've got a head start. Do some in-person interviewing. Try to locate some unmarried kids who've gotten pregnant while still in school and talk to them about their choices. See if you can talk with someone who's had an abortion as well as someone who's had the child and released it for adoption. Try to talk with someone who is raising a baby and has stayed in school herself. If you can't easily do these things, call a health center that advertises abortion and family planning services and see what they have to say. You might also try calling a pro-life center that suggests alternatives other than abortion. Take notes as you talk. Later on, reread your notes but with the understanding that each position comes with a particular bias. . . .

Whatever you choose to do, it must be an informed choice and it must reflect your own needs. You don't need to isolate yourself or hide in shame. This isn't Puritan America and you're not Hester Prynne walking around with a scarlet letter on your dress. Making a mistake doesn't brand you forever, and there are many people out there who will help you without judging you or pressuring you to do something you don't want to do. . . .

An Informed Choice

Discussing options and making decisions shouldn't turn into a battle for control over the outcome of a pregnancy. Think of the discussion as similar to buying an insurance policy—you need to look at lots of programs before finding the one that suits you best, even if the process is tedious, confusing, and sometimes scary. That insurance policy is designed to protect you and make your life more secure. Finding the correct option you and your family can live with comfortably will do the same.

An unplanned pregnancy does not have to signal the end of your world or doom you to a life-style you don't want to live. It can actually become a catalyst for positive change—the event that gets you and your family talking or helps you develop a more realistic view of life, something that pushes you to acknowledge your strengths and use them in solving your problem. It is also an event that forces you to come to terms with the power of your sexuality and what can happen if you are careless with it. The bottom line is that you are in charge of your sexuality; the choices are yours. Try to make them informed choices based on accurate facts.

a critical thinking activity

The Ability
To Empathize

In this activity you will be asked to struggle with some of the questions a pregnant teenager must face. Should the young woman have an abortion? Give the baby up for adoption? Keep the child? Should other people have a say in what the teenager decides? These and other ethical questions arise every time a teen unexpectedly becomes pregnant. Religious background, personal philosophy, and life experiences all become factors in making such decisions.

This exercise is designed to improve your problem-solving skills through empathizing: the ability to understand situations from another's point of view. After reading the viewpoints in this chapter, the class should break into groups of five or six people. Each student should read the scenario below and take the role of a person involved in the teenager's decisionmaking process. The group members should present their arguments on what to do about the pregnancy from the perspective of the characters selected.

The Situation

Sarah is an average American high school student. She is a 17-year-old senior who gets good grades and is a member of the track team. In addition to school, Sarah works 15 hours a week and is saving for college which she hopes to attend the coming fall. She is also pregnant.

Sarah's mother, who is quite religious, has warned her about premarital sex. She will be very disappointed when she finds out about Sarah's pregnancy, but would never advocate abortion. Sarah's father, on the other hand, does not want anything to prevent Sarah from getting a college degree. Sarah knows that, realistically, she can neither start college in an advanced state of pregnancy nor continue full-time classes while trying to raise and support a child.

Sarah does not want to marry the father nor does she assume that he will provide much support should she decide to keep the child. Sarah must make a decision on her own.

The Roles

Sarah: must decide what to do about her pregnancy and how it will affect her future.

Sarah's mother: believes abortion is immoral and would like to see Sarah give the baby up for adoption.

Sarah's father: thinks Sarah should to go college and therefore have an abortion.

a friend: dropped out of school after becoming pregnant and keeping the child. She wants Sarah to have an abortion and attend college.

the school counselor: wants Sarah to make an informed decision of her own free will.

Sarah's boyfriend: does not want to marry Sarah nor support the child, but wants Sarah to keep the child so that he can see it grow up.

Discussion

In your groups, have each person try to convince Sarah that their solution is the best alternative. Present as many arguments as possible from each character's perspective. After all the group members have expressed their opinions, Sarah must decide what to do about the pregnancy based on what she believes is the most convincing argument. When the student playing Sarah has made a decision, stay in your group and discuss the following questions:

1. What are the most compelling reasons for keeping the child? For puttting it up for adoption? For having an abortion?
2. What are the most compelling arguments against each option?
3. Was Sarah's decision more difficult to make than that of a pregnant, unwed 25-year-old woman who lives on her own? Why or why not?
4. How much influence did economics and parental authority have on Sarah's decision?

Periodical Bibliography

The following articles have been selected to supplement the diverse views presented in this chapter.

Elizabeth Rice Allgeier	"'Are You Ready for Sex?': Informed Consent for Sexual Intimacy," *SIECUS Report*, July 1985.
Christianity Today	"Can States Restrict a Minor's Access to Abortion?" April 3, 1987.
David Gates	"Blowing the Whistle on the Squeal Rule," *Newsweek*, September 24, 1984.
Jet	"Pregnant Teens Must Make Own Choices on Abortion," July 14, 1986.
Barbara Kantrowitz	"Teenagers and Abortion," *Newsweek*, October 12, 1987.
Cheryl McCall	"Denise's Decision," *Life*, March 1986.
Kate Manning	"Am I Old Enough To Be a Parent?" *Redbook*, May 1987.
Hattie-Jo P. Mullins	"The Rocky Courtship of Teens and Birth Control," *Ms.*, March 1987.
Hyman Rodman	"Controlling Adolescent Fertility," *Society*, November/December 1985.
Michael Satchell	"Abortion: Once More to the Fore," *U.S. News & World Report*, September 7, 1987.
Kenneth Slack	"The Doctor and the Underage Girl," *The Christian Century*, February 20, 1985.
Faye Wattleton	"Reproductive Rights for a More Humane World," *The Humanist*, July/August 1986.

Organizations To Contact

The editors have compiled the following list of organizations which are concerned with the issues debated in this book. All of them have publications available for interested readers. The descriptions are derived from materials provided by the organizations themselves.

Alan Guttmacher Institute (AGI)
111 5th Ave.
New York, NY 10003
(212) 254-5827

AGI works to develop adequate family planning and sex education programs through policy analysis, public education, and research. The Institute publishes the bimonthly *Family Planning Perspectives* and the quarterly *International Family Planning Perspectives*.

American Civil Liberties Union (ACLU)
132 W. 43rd St.
New York, NY 10036
(212) 944-9899

The ACLU champions the rights set forth in the Declaration of Independence and the US Constitution, including the right to a safe and legal abortion for all women. It publishes a monthly newsletter, *First Principles*, and a bimonthly newspaper, *Civil Liberties*.

American Life League
PO Box 1350
Stafford, VA 22554
(703) 546-5550

The League serves as a pro-life service organization providing educational materials and programs for pro-life, pro-family organizations. It publishes a monthly, *Levers of Power*, a study, *School Birth Control: New Promise for an Old Problem*, and various brochures.

Americans United for Life
343 S. Dearborn St., Suite 1804
Chicago, IL 60604
(312) 786-9494

This organization is an educational and legal pro-life group. It operates the Americans United for Life Legal Defense Fund and a legal resource center on abortion. It publishes a quarterly newsletter, *Lex Vitae*.

Center for Population Options
2031 Florida Ave. NW
Washington, DC 20009
(202) 387-5091

The Center provides sex education to promote sexual responsibility among teenagers. It publishes two quarterlies, *Population Options* and *Issues and Action Update*.

Children's Defense Fund
122 C St. NW
Washington, DC 20001
(202) 628-8787

This organization is a national children's advocacy group working for the rights and protection of children. Its Adolescent Pregnancy Prevention Clearinghouse publishes six reports per year on America's teen pregnancy crisis and its solutions.

Concerned Women for America
122 C St. NW, Suite 800
Washington, DC 20001
(202) 628-3014

This group works to strengthen the traditional family according to Judeo-Christian moral standards. It publishes several brochures, including *Teen Pregnancy and School-Based Health Clinics.*

Couple to Couple League
PO Box 11084
Cincinnati, OH 45211
(513) 661-7612

The League teaches natural family planning methods and opposes artificial contraception, premarital sex, and abortion. It publishes a bimonthly newsletter, *CCL News,* and *The Art of Natural Family Planning* manual. Also available is *The Springtime of Your Life,* a pro-chastity slide show for teens.

Eagle Forum
PO Box 618
Alton, IL 62002
(618) 462-5415

Eagle Forum is dedicated to preserving traditional family values based on the Bible. It is against premarital sex and abortion. The group publishes the *Phyllis Schlafly Report,* a monthly newsletter.

Human Life Center
University of Steubenville
Steubenville, OH 43952
(614) 282-9953

The Center teaches natural family planning and conservative Roman Catholic moral values regarding sex, marriage, and family. It publishes two quarterlies, *International Review of Natural Family Planning* and *Human Life Issues.*

National Abortion Federation
900 Pennsylvania Ave. SE
Washington, DC 20003
(202) 546-9060

The Federation is a political action group dedicated to sustaining a pro-choice political constituency in order to maintain the right to a legal abortion for all women. It publishes the *NARAL Newsletter* quarterly.

National Family Planning and Reproductive Health Association, Inc.
122 C St. NW, Suite 380
Washington, DC 20001
(202) 628-3535

The Association works to improve family planning and reproductive health services by acting as a national communications network. It publishes *NFPRHA News* and *Report* monthly, as well as various papers including "The Effects of Sexuality Education," "Implementing a Young Man's Sexuality Education Program," and "Clinic and Contraceptive Use of Adolescent Clients."

National Right to Life Committee
419 7th St. NW, Suite 402
Washington, DC 20004
(202) 626-8800

The Committee is a pro-life organization which supports alternative programs in counseling and adoption, provides public education on pro-life issues, and lobbies before Congress for a Human Rights Amendment. It publishes *National Right to Life News* biweekly, and many pamphlets, including *Challenge To Be Pro-Life*.

National Urban League, Inc.
500 E. 62nd St.
New York, NY 10021
(212) 310-9000

The Urban League is a leading civil rights organization that works to ensure equal opportunity for socially and economically disadvantaged persons. It currently conducts three national programs addressing adolescent pregnancy and parenting. It publishes the quarterly *Urban League News* as well as *Community Surveys and Reports* on an irregular basis.

Office of Population Affairs
US Department of Health and Human Services
Room 736-E
200 Independence Ave. SW
Washington, DC 20201
(202) 245-0142

The Office of Population Affairs is a division of the Department of Health and Human Services, a Cabinet-level agency which creates and monitors social policies and programs. Its publications include a fact sheet titled *The Family and Adolescent Pregnancy*.

Planned Parenthood
810 7th Ave.
New York, NY 10019
(212) 541-7800

Planned Parenthood supports people making their own decisions about having children without governmental interference. They provide contraceptive counseling and services through clinics located throughout the US. Among their extensive publications are the brochures, *Guide to Birth Control: Seven Accepted Methods of Contraception, Teensex? It's OK to Say No Way, A Man's Guide to Sexuality,* and *About Childbirth*. Write for a free catalog of publications.

Project Respect
PO Box 39
Golf, IL 60029-0039
(312) 729-3298

Project Respect was created by a concerned parent as a response to public school sex education curricula which focused on contraception as the primary means of preventing teen pregnancy. The Project distributes a sex education curriculum, *Sex Respect*, which encourages sexual abstinence as the best method of pregnancy prevention.

Search Institute
122 W. Franklin Ave., Suite 525
Minneapolis, MN 55404-9990
(612) 870-9511

The Institute is a research organization which provides information and programs about adolescents and family life to social service professionals. Its programs encourage traditional family and sexual values. It publishes a sex education curriculum for junior high school students and their parents, *Human Sexuality: Values and Choices.*

Sex Information and Education Council of the US (SIECUS)
80 5th Ave., Suite 801
New York, NY 10011
(212) 929-2300

SIECUS is one of the largest national clearinghouses for information on sexuality. In addition to publishing sex education curricula, SIECUS also publishes a newsletter, *SIECUS Report*, and the books, *Adolescent Pregnancy and Parenthood* and *Oh No! What Do I Do Now?*

Teen-Aid
W. 22 Mission
Spokane, WA 99201
(509) 466-8679

Teen-Aid is an international organization which promotes traditional family values and sexual morality. It publishes a public school sex education curriculum, *Sexuality, Commitment and Family*, stressing sexual abstinence before marriage.

Bibliography of Books

Joan Wester Anderson — *Teen Is a Four-Letter Word*. White Hall, VA: Betterway Publications, 1983.

Dave Andrusko, ed. — *Window on the Future*. Washington, DC: National Right to Life Committee, 1986.

Lawrence Bauman with Robert Riche — *The Nine Most Troublesome Teenage Problems*. Secaucus, NJ: Lyle Stuart Inc., 1986.

Ruth Bell and Leni Zeiger Wildflower — *Talking with Your Teenager: A Book for Parents*. New York: Random House, 1984.

Paul Borthwick — *But You Don't Understand*. Nashville, TN: Thomas Nelson Publishers, 1986.

Robert Coles and Geoffrey Stokes — *Sex and the American Teenager*. New York: Harper & Row, 1985.

John Janeway Conger and Anne C. Peterson — *Adolescence and Youth*. New York: Harper & Row, 1984.

Glenbard East Echo — *Teenagers Themselves*. New York: Adama Books, 1984.

Frederick Elkin and Gerald Handel — *The Child and Society*. New York: Random House, 1984.

Jerry Falwell — *If I Should Die Before I Wake*. Nashville, TN: Thomas Nelson Publishers, 1986.

Harold Feldman and Andrea Parrot — *Human Sexuality: Contemporary Controversies*. Beverly Hills, CA: Sage, 1984.

Frank F. Furstenberg Jr., J. Brooks-Gunn, and S. Philip Morgan — *Adolescent Mothers in Later Life*. New York: Cambridge University Press, 1987.

Jay Gale — *A Young Man's Guide to Sex*. New York: Holt, Rinehart and Winston, 1984.

James Geer, Julia Heiman, and Harold Leitenberg — *Human Sexuality*. Englewood Cliffs, NJ: Prentice-Hall, 1984.

Sol Gordon and Judith Gordon — *Raising a Child Conservatively in a Sexually Permissive World*. New York: Simon & Schuster, 1983.

Tipper Gore — *Raising PG Kids in an X-Rated Society*. Nashville, TN: Abingdon Press, 1987.

Cheryl D. Hayes, ed. — *Risking the Future: Adolescent Sexuality, Pregnancy, and Childbearing*. Washington, DC: National Academy Press, 1987.

Douglas Kirby — *School-Based Health Clinics*. Washington, DC: Center for Population Options, 1985.

Robert C. Kolodny, Nancy J. Kolodny, Thomas Bratter, and Cheryl Deep — *How To Survive Your Adolescent's Adolescence*. Boston: Little, Brown and Co., 1984.

Jane Lancaster and Beatrix Hamburg — *School-Age Pregnancy and Parenthood*. Hawthorne, NY: Aldine de Gruyter, 1985.

Sharon R. Lovick — *School-Based Clinics: Update*. Washington, DC: Center for Population Options, 1987.

Lynda Madaras with Dane Saavedra — *The 'What's Happening to My Body?' Book for Boys.* New York: Newmarket Press, 1984.

Rita Marker — *Shaping the Future: A Report on School Based Clinics,* 1987. Available from the Human Life Center, University of Steubenville, Steubenville, OH 43952.

Coleen Kelly Mast — *Love and Life.* Bradley, IL: Respect Inc., 1986.

William A. Masters, Virginia E. Johnson, and Robert C. Kolodny — *Sex and Human Loving.* Boston: Little, Brown and Co., 1986.

Gary B. Melton, ed. — *Adolescent Abortion.* Lincoln, NE: University of Nebraska Press, 1986.

Gary B. Melton, Gerald P. Koocher, and Michael J. Saks — *Children's Competence To Consent.* New York: Plenum Press, 1983.

Lois B. Morris — *Talking Sex.* New York: Simon & Schuster, 1984.

Barrett Mosbacker — *Teen Pregnancy and School-Based Health Clinics,* 1986. Available from the Family Research Council, 515 Second St. NE, Washington, DC 20002.

Lesley Jane Nonkin — *I Wish My Parents Understood.* New York: Freundlich Books, 1985.

Sally Wendkos Olds — *The Eternal Garden: Seasons of Our Sexuality.* New York: Random House, 1985.

Douglas H. Powell — *Teenagers: When To Worry and What To Do.* Garden City, NY: Doubleday, 1986.

Marilyn Ratner and Susan Chamlin — *Straight Talk.* White Plains, NY: Planned Parenthood, 1985.

Arlene Kramer Richards and Irene Willis — *Under 18 and Pregnant.* New York: Lothrop, Lee, and Shephard Books, 1983.

Hyman Rodman — *The Adolescent Dilemma.* New York: Praeger, 1986.

Phyllis Schlafly — *Child Abuse in the Classroom.* Alton, IL: Pere Marquette Press, 1984.

Max Sugar, ed. — *Adolescent Parenthood.* New York: Spectrum Publications, 1984.

Susan K. Sullivan and Matthre A. Kawiak — *Parents Talk Love.* New York: Paulist Press, 1985.

Jacqueline Voss and Jay Gale — *A Young Woman's Guide to Sex.* New York: Henry Holt and Co., 1986.

Oralee Wachter — *Sex, Drugs, & AIDS.* New York: Bantam, 1987.

Elizabeth A. Weisman and Michael H. Weisman — *What We Told Our Kids About Sex.* San Diego: Harcourt Brace Jovanovich, 1987.

Nancy Fugate Woods — *Human Sexuality in Health and Illness.* St. Louis, MO: The C.V. Mosby Company, 1984.

Phyllis York, David York, and Ted Wachtel — *Toughlove Solutions.* Garden City, NY: Doubleday, 1984.

Index

213

119-120
and sex education, 52-53, 57-58, 62, 77
Muraskin, Lana D., 47

Neuhaus, Richard John, 117

parents
  and abortion, 186-189, 191-194
  and contraception, 97-98, 116, 158
  effects on teenage sexuality, 56-60, 68, 121
  rights of, 183-184
  should control teen sexuality, 186-189, 196-198
  should not control teen sexuality, 191-194, 200-203
  should teach sex ed, 56-60, 117
    con, 44, 48, 62-63, 70, 79
  support school-based health clinics, 110-111, 126
    con, 114, 119-122, 176
Parrot, Andrea, 21, 30
Pasman, Jo Ellen, 192
Peirce, Neal R., 125
Pett, Joel, 74
Pittman, Karen J., 149
pornography, 35-37
Powell, Lane H., 63
pregnancy, teenage, 135-169
  and poverty, 18-20, 136-137, 152
  and race, 18-20, 137
  causes for, 44, 146
    lack of self-esteem, 182
    quitting school, 148
    school-based health clinics, 95, 98
    unsupervised teens, 147
  costs of, 81-82, 178, 182
  rates of, 95, 124, 127
    are epidemic, 135-139, 152
      con, 141-144, 178
    effects on
      education, 98
      contraception, 98
  solutions
    contraception, 105, 143, 158-162
      will not work, 101, 164-169
    educational programs, 98, 146-150
    parental notification laws, 186, 189
      con, 192, 193
    pay teens to remain childless, 152-156
    school-based health clinics, 105, 108-112, 124-128, 149, 160
      will not work, 120-121
    traditional values, 77, 101, 114-117

see also contraception; school-based health clinics
premarital sex, see abstinence, sexual; sexual activity, teenage

Quinlan, Maura K., 185

reproductive health services
  and morality, 20-22
  US policy toward, 20-21
reproductive rights
  parents should control, 186-189, 196-198
  teens should control, 191-194, 200-203
Ritter, Bruce, 36
Rodman, Hyman, 66
Rosen, Hy, 136

safe sex, 18, 73-74, 101, 102
St. Paul Maternal and Infant Care Project, 105, 108-109, 114, 125
Schlafly, Phyllis, 98, 184
school-based health clinics, 90-128
  and abortion, 95, 96, 110, 121
  and contraception, 90-91, 92, 104, 176
  and morality, 115-117, 119-120
  are effective, 90-93
  are ineffective, 95-99
  effects of
    encourage sexual activity, 101-102, 114-115
      con, 91, 104-106
    increase teen pregnancies, 95, 98
    reduce teen pregnancies, 92-93, 124-125, 149
  parental opposition to, 114, 119-122, 176
  parental support for, 110-111, 126
Schwartz, Michael, 25
sex education, 44-83
  and abortion, 52-53
  and mass media, 33, 44-45
  and morality, 22, 52-53, 57-58, 62, 77
  and sexual abuse, 64
  increases sexual activity, 52-53
    con, 22, 71, 79-81
  is harmful, 50-54
  is inadequate, 57, 59, 81
  is ineffective, 45-46
  is necessary, 44-48, 67-71
  should be taught at home, 56-60, 117
    con, 44, 48, 62-63, 70, 79
  should be taught in church, 62-65

214

215